REMEMBERING SLATON TEXAS

On the desolate plains, about 1911, the Slaton Post Office serviced the few residents who arrived early. *Photo from the Slaton Town Square Antique Mall and Museum.*

REMEMBERING SLATON ★ TEXAS ★

Centennial Stories, 1911–2011

James Villanueva

The History PRESS

Published by The History Press
Charleston, SC 29403
www.historypress.net

Cover logo designed by Nathan Emerson.

First published 2011

Manufactured in the United States

ISBN 978.1.60949.243.4

Library of Congress Cataloging-in-Publication Data

Villanueva, James.
Remembering Slaton, Texas : centennial stories, 1911-2011 / James Villanueva.
p. cm.
Includes index.
ISBN 978-1-60949-243-4
1. Slaton (Tex.)--History--Anecdotes. 2. Slaton (Tex.)--Biography--Anecdotes. 3. Slaton (Tex.)--Social life and customs--Anecdotes. 4. Slaton (Tex.)--Anniversaries, etc. I. Title.
F394.S58V45 2011
976.4'847--dc22
2011008303

To Steve Villanueva

Contents

Foreword, by Jim Davis 9
Acknowledgements 11

The Assignment, 2010 13
Boomtown, 1911 19
The Pember Family, 1915 26
Annie Schuette's Story, 2010 31
The Flip of a Switch, 1920 34
The Tar and Feathering of Father Keller, 1922 45
Movies in Slaton, 1920 52
Edna Walter's Story, 2010 55
The Dust Bowl Era, 1920s 58
A Tale of Two Railroad Cities, 1927 67
Love in the Time of Influenza, 1932 70
A Father's Journey, 1932 78
Cecil Scott's Story, 2008 81
Remembering Grandpa, 2010 84
Slaton's History of Death, 1912 87
Ysaura Flores's Story, 2009 90
The Ladies of the Civic Culture Club, 1939 93
The War Years, 1941–1945 97

The Slaton Bakery, 1943 105
Across the Great Plains, 1943 109
Lights Out for the Forrest Hotel, 1953 113
A Shooting in Pleasant Valley, 1961 116
The Slaton Situation, 1961 119
Slaton in '63 122
Slaton's Boy, 2009 125
The Class of 1968 128
Coffee Talk at the Auto Shop, 2009 133

Index 137
About the Author 143

Foreword

Slaton, Texas, has lived one hundred years, into which civilization has jammed more history and growth than in all the time that came before. From the height of the railroad era through the automobile and the airplane ages to space exploration; from the War to End All Wars through the greatest generation's war to a Facebook revolution in Egypt; from the bubble of the Roaring Twenties through the Great Depression to the great recession; from the hint of radio through transistors to microchips, Slaton has lived its life.

Its life is the story told in James Villanueva's *Remembering Slaton, Texas: Centennial Stories, 1911–2011*. His is the story of life behind the great events of ordinary people coming to West Texas with the railroad, coming to West Texas to farm, coming to West Texas looking for something better—some to succeed, some to fail. His is the story of dreams and celebrations, hardships and tragedies, the events of everyday existence. His story is real history drawn from the history told by those who lived it, recorded in the archives and reported in *The Slatonite*.

His story is the texture around which an extraordinary century flowed. His is a great story.

Jim Davis
Editor-Publisher
The Slatonite

Acknowledgements

There are many people who helped this project go from idea to reality. The first person I want to thank is my publisher and editor at *The Slatonite*, Jim Davis, for trusting me with this assignment, and Yvonne Green for her brilliant editing. I would also like to thank the publishing house The History Press and my commissioning editor, Becky LeJeune, for the support, encouragement and patience it took to make this book possible. I would like to thank Mark Meurer for encouraging me to write about the history of Slaton. Also helping to make this book possible were Jolene Fondy, Cindy Moore, Alton Kenney and John Westefeld, whose tireless efforts of maintaining the heritage and culture of Slaton are inspirational in their own right. I must also thank Becky Ford for trusting me with an endless amount of time at the Town Square Antique Mall and Museum. I also want to thank my friends D'Etta Brown, Jackye and Johnny Neal, Kerry Kerns, Kris Galvan, Chris Shumaker and David Ariaz for providing listening ears and, at times, a break from history. I also want to thank my good friend Rod Rodriguez for providing a weekend escape from the countless hours of research and writing. Of course, none of this could have been possible without my family, a colorful group of people who first taught me the gift of storytelling by the endless amounts of narratives told at family dinners and on holidays. But most of all, I must give credit to the people of Slaton, who honestly and bravely opened their hearts and, whether in their homes or in line at the grocery store, trusted me with their stories—their histories.

The Assignment, 2010

It was a humbling experience when my publisher at *The Slatonite* newspaper in Slaton, Texas, Jim Davis, pulled me aside in the office one day and told me it was time to prepare for the centennial celebration of this little town, and it would be my duty to write the town's history.

A million questions raced through my head. A million concerns pulsed through my body. After all, this town of only six thousand people at the roughest estimates was just one diminutive part of my three-year plan.

This was not my lot in life. This was not my calling. This was not my passion. Slaton was just a town where I was recharging before the true realities of post-college life began. Nothing more.

Jim's office was cluttered with regional magazines and books about aviation and politics. A computer blared before him, and various pieces of scrap paper with scribbles on them blanketed the large desk.

"We need something every week," he said in his slow voice, with the hint of a Dallas accent that was different and a bit more sophisticated than the West Texas drawl that swathed our small newspaper office, where people came in every day to place garage sale announcements or classified advertisements selling hay.

"Alright," I said, scribbling notes on a yellow pad. "So a story every week on something historical about the town." I wrote down every word he said, trying to decipher the assignment with each stroke of my black pen.

"Nothing big," he said. "Just a little something to keep the town interested."

"Did anything good ever happen in this town?" My sarcastic tongue got the best of me again.

Typical housing on the prairie, Roy Meeks built this home in 1916. In the picture, a young Alton Meeks rides a horse as his brother, Robert, and mother, Sue, watch. *Photo from the Slaton Town Square Antique Mall and Museum.*

"We'll start running it this week," he said with a brief chuckle. That chuckle was my cue to leave, as he picked up a phone and began dialing.

I made my way to my computer, and there, with my cursor taunting me from the empty computer screen, I slowly began typing—then backspaced each word and began again. I leaned back in my chair and thought, Where to start?

I could have easily begun at the point when the deeds of Slaton were signed over in 1910, making Slaton more than one hundred years old during that spring of 2010. Of course, I had to also give respect to the people who first settled the land in the 1540s. History has shown that the Apache, Comanche and Kiowa people once roamed the area. Didn't those people matter? They were, after all, partly responsible for helping to make this land inhabitable. Because of the intense heat, lack of water and extreme weather patterns, as well as the continual tribal warfare, the land was no place for European settlers.

Of course, the area is part of the vast South Plains, and this fair town is merely a minuscule part of the land. A tiny dot on a map, Slaton is located in north-central Texas. It is on the Double Mountain Fork of the Brazos River,

Texas Avenue, circa 1924. *Photo from the Slaton Town Square Antique Mall and Museum.*

near the eastern edge of the Llano Estacada, which is considered one of the world's flattest areas.

In the early 1900s, throughout the sprawling country, people continued moving westward, finding their way by buggy, train and the newly invented automobile to California and all points in between, including to a rumored new town formed by the Santa Fe Railroad Line: Slaton.

Sometime between 1909 and 1910, tents sprung up along the railroad on the north end of where present-day Slaton Town Square now sits.

For months, people waited as a town formed. They waited for new opportunities and a new future, never truly knowing what would come out of this barren land that was once considered squalid by Spaniard standards. They never knew, as they sat waiting, of all the stories, achievements, successes and, of course, tragedies that generations of Slatonites squandered away in little boxes, scrapbooks, yearbooks and letters that would be left behind for me to discover more than one hundred years later.

Of course, everything I know about history has been passed down to me from stories, pictures and distilled images of the small arsenal of video footage shot throughout even modern-day history. "Tent City, 1910" is just a grainy image, as are most photos I stumbled upon during my many hours of research. Everything in the past, it seemed, happened moments before I was born. I must trust those people who were there, the people who saw it happen and lived it.

I have nothing else.

So, as I leaned back and thought about my responsibilities of documenting this town's history, I thought about how this year, this tiny year of the past one hundred, just might be larger than me, and I am extremely fortunate to be here, at this moment, remembering the ones that brought me to this place, honoring those who helped make it happen.

ONIE BAXLEY'S STORY, 2010

In preparation for my yearlong journey into the history of Slaton, I had to speak with someone who was there at the beginning. Not necessarily the beginning of the town, but the beginning of the 1900s.

Onie Baxley, although one of Slaton's newest residents (she moved to the town in 1997), is also one of its wisest. After celebrating her 101st birthday in 2010, I picked up my pen and yellow notepad and raced down to the Slaton Care Center Retirement Home to hear her story, in her words.

Baxley's story is that of death, heartache and, every so often, glimpses of hope that moved people forward in a black-and-white world.

"I was born June 19, 1909," she said, sipping from a cup filled with Dr Pepper, which she gripped in her right hand while staring out at the courtyard of the care center. "Do you like my watch?" she asked, lifting her small wrist as if it were weighted down by dumbbells, showing me the pale pink watch sparkling with rhinestones given to her by a grandchild who joined her in celebration of her 101st year.

"It's beautiful," I yelled into her ear. Throughout the years, her hearing had slowly slipped away. I felt awful having to yell at her, but it was the only way we could communicate.

We sat together, just the two of us, a smile as big as the moon creeping across her face.

"You're a nice young man," she said. My cold, harsh demeanor as an objective reporter melted away. My shoulders relaxed. She continued smiling.

"Thanks," I yelled again.

Onie pointed to a place next to her bed. I followed her small, shaky finger, and my eyes landed on a blue photo album. I reached over and grabbed it from the desk propped neatly against her bed, as if reading her mind. She said, "Yes."

Passing the album to her, she reached out, and I helped her place her glass of Dr Pepper on a table in front of her.

Surrounding us, I noticed all the family photographs. "Let me help you," I said. She stared at me, blank. "Help you!" I yelled. She opened the album.

"This is my mom," she said, smiling again. In the album was a worn photo of a woman in a floral dress. The regal woman looked out of the photo placed firmly on Onie's lap. "I was born June 19, 1909," she said, continuing her story in her soft voice. "My mother died a few weeks later. My dad told me they were visiting my oldest sister, Lola, to see her first baby. They got ready to go home. She started riding in a buggy, and she died in my dad's arms on the way to their home."

I stared at the picture, trying my hardest to remember the image of the young woman who had brought Mrs. Baxley into this world. I looked to see Onie doing the same.

Onie continued telling me stories of when she was a child, stories that involved horses, the occasional wild wolf and her eleven siblings, who helped rear her after her mother died. In my head, however, I tried remembering the woman from the picture, who, even more than one hundred years later,

Before the trains, Slaton was a vast prairie surrounded by canyons, such as the Horseshoe Bend Canyon on the south side of the city. Circa 1910. *Photo from the Slaton Town Square Antique Mall and Museum.*

continued helping Onie find sleep in a new century—a mother she never knew but with whom she began her "100 Years in the Making" story.

"It was nice meeting you," she said after telling me her tale. "You're a really nice young man." The familiar smile spread across her face. For a moment, I smiled back as the hot summer sun raged through the window.

I leaned down and yelled, "Thanks for telling me your story!" into her ear, as if shouting into a canyon and hoping to hear an echo.

"In life," she said, as if now reading my mind, "there's a lot of heartache, but you just—" She stared out the window once more. "I'm sorry," she said. "My mind just isn't what it used to be."

Boomtown, 1911

On that hot summer day, June 15, 1911, they arrived.

It is written, in various historical articles and documents, that on that hot and dry summer day, typical to most West Texas summers, people came by horse and buggy, by team and wagon, by train and on foot to a new town in hopes of new opportunities.

On a special excursion train, J.F. Utter of Amarillo was the first conductor to bring passengers to the city of Slaton. For the first time that day, many heard the familiar sounds of train whistles blowing across West Texas skies.

Some brought lunches, and with their families in tow, beneath "improvised shade by means of wagon sheets and tar-paulins, they ate in the hot sun or under sparse shade of the mesquite trees," Reverend Lowell C. Green wrote in a 1953 issue of *The Slatonite*. He was the former Lutheran pastor of Slaton.

According to Green's research, the crowd gathered early and included many prominent railroad officials, some of whom had come from as far as Topeka, Kansas.

On that afternoon, land lots were sold to Slaton's first citizens.

Of course, the planning of the event that took place that summer day had begun years prior on a small farm surrounded by a great and vast field, where, aside from a coyote yelp in the night or the chirping of cicadas, deafening silence overtook much of the Texas plains in the late 1800s—before the trains.

On September 1, 1879, the original town site of the future city of Slaton was patented by the State of Texas to Eli Stilson and J.I. Case. The land was located on Survey 41 and Survey 44. The site was later sold to the Western Land and Livestock Company.

This transaction led to the great 10A Ranch being sold to J.W. Kokernot and H.L. Kokernot. It is believed that settlement on the land thrived because of the Kokernots, and soon the land was sold, once again, to J.C. Phillips. During this time, Santa Fe Railway was in the early stages of buying land for a projected town in West Texas.

The Santa Fe Railway Company was making progress in providing countrywide train transportation. Within this area, there was a need for a division point with facilities for servicing the trains. Since the land for the town site had been established, representatives of the Santa Fe turned to the task of establishing a city.

The city of Slaton was named after local rancher and banker O.L. Slaton. *Photo from* Slaton's Story.

According to various documents, the sale transaction of the town site was completed on April 15, 1911. E.B. Storey Jr. was sent from Chicago by the Santa Fe Railway to buy land for the projected town. The Pecos and Northern Texas Railway Company of the Santa Fe system proposed to create a new division point and city in its newly acquired plot.

The town was to be named after local rancher O.L. Slaton, and the plot layout would duplicate that of Washington, D.C.—a pinwheel-style downtown.

On May 11, 1911, the streets and alleyways of Slaton were dedicated in a document to the public. The first people to arrive in Slaton stayed in tents, while buildings and houses bloomed around them. According to Green, preparation for the opening day included a very ambitious advertising program. Printed circulars, describing the lay of the land and promising ample water, were distributed up and down the Santa Fe system from Lubbock to Kansas.

Vyola Hubbard, one of the first settlers in Slaton, wrote in an essay in 1979:

> *To be young in a young town is something quite unique and altogether different from being young in a town that was old when you were born. The people were mostly youthful—full of confidence. Those daring that*

The Thomas Logan Reed family, like many others, made their way to church on horse and buggy, which was common at the time. Circa 1919. *Photo from* Slaton's Story.

> *the horse and buggy were growing old, and beginning to fade, would not have risked leaving their comfortable homes and lives for the uncertainty of a boomtown.*

So it was that on that hot summer day, June 15, 1911, they arrived. A boomtown was born.

DR. NICHOLS ARRIVES, 1911

Come on and hear,
Come on and hear,
Alexander's Ragtime Band.

When E.O. Nichols, MD, arrived in New York by train, he remembered the sounds of Alexander's Ragtime Band playing in a New York City beer garden. It was, after all, the biggest hit of 1911.

The music was upbeat, but according to historians, hardships were aplenty as the world entered a new century, and Dr. Nichols started a new life in a city overflowing with immigrants. While at the beer garden, it is easy to imagine Nichols swapping stories of being the first doctor in Slaton.

President William Taft was in office, the Philadelphia Athletics were on their way to winning the World Series and the city of Slaton was dedicated to the public.

It was 1911 when Dr. Nichols departed for New York City after a brief stay in Slaton. Nichols gave detailed description of this time in his book, *Medicine and Cowboys Sixty Years Ago and Today's Politics*. The book was published in February 1969.

Practicing in Slaton for only three months, Nichols offered a vivid account of the new town, and it remains one of the earliest writings featuring the birth of this particular boomtown.

In an essay written in 1979 about the early years of Slaton, Slatonite Vyola Hubbard wrote:

> *There was only one doctor in town—Dr. Nichols. Dr. Adams had not yet arrived* [in Slaton]. *Dr. Nichols was so young he had to grow a beard to look professional—but when it came to medical knowledge he was really*

> *way out in front. He* [Nichols] *had been trained in the new ways that were to open up an amazing and marvelous world of medicine thru the first half of the twentieth century.*

Nichols wrote in his book that when he arrived in Slaton, most people lived in tents.

Nichols recalled the price of lots in the new town as $300 each, and in three days the price increased to $2,200. "A man would tell a lot owner I will give you a hundred dollars more than you paid—and prices went up and up." He also recalled that one man paid $300 for a lot, and when the price reached $1,400, he took his profit and left for another town.

Making camp in a tent at first, Nichols eventually decided to build a small barn for Old Dobbin, his horse. His wife agreed to move in (she was staying with her mother in Lubbock), if they could get a stove and a little furniture.

"My wife moved in to feed me some food that was not contaminated by flies," Nichols wrote.

> [The barn] *had a dirt floor and a hole in the wall for a window. While I was out making a night call, one of those wonderful little friends, a burro, stuck his head through the window and let out one of those long-drawn-out noises that will shake the rafters. My wife was in bed when the big noise started and in two seconds she was under the bed. We decided to build a little two-room house.*

Dr. Nichols's office was located behind the first drugstore in town, Red Cross Pharmacy. It is believed the pharmacy was located at 109 South Ninth Street, the site of the current Slaton Bakery.

As people migrated to Slaton, Dr. Nichols wrote that he treated hundreds of patients in his three months there. He charged residents twenty dollars for his service, and yet a few citizens complained that his fees were too high considering they could use a midwife for five dollars.

With the money he was receiving, Nichols eventually bought a horse and buggy for seventy-five dollars.

Nichols wrote about his hectic business of being the lone doctor in a boomtown: "I was busy doing everything from setting fractures, and suturing cuts from fights, to extracting teeth."

At the end of his three-month stay, however, Nichols wrote that his services were becoming more and more taxing, thus making life that much more complicated for him and his wife.

Then, one night, a man arrived at his office after riding in from nine miles east of the town site.

"He said his wife had a miscarriage and was hemorrhaging," Nichols wrote.

> *I was following him in the dark, and the first thing I knew the buggy was on an incline and turned over—spilling me, my medicine case and instruments over the side. The horse was so frightened he did not move. The cowboy helped me turn the buggy upright, collect my medical case and instruments.*

Dr. Nichols arrived at the house and found an extremely ill woman. He wrote that she had bled until he could no longer find a pulse. The cowboy left Nichols to aid his wife while he rode to a local rancher's house to phone in a doctor from Floydada. Dr. Adams arrived early the next morning. Both Nichols and Adams curetted the woman and removed the afterbirth. The woman's pulse stabilized, and Drs. Adams and Nichols returned to their respective offices—Nichols in Slaton and Adams in Floydada.

Three days later, the cowboy returned to Nichols's office and said that his wife had delivered a child. "Why didn't you tell me she was going to have a chill [child]?" the man demanded.

"Hell, I didn't know she would have a chill," Dr. Nichols told the man. He returned to the house, where Nichols helped the woman deliver a second child. The first was sick from infections.

Nichols stayed for two days and nights and aided the ailing twins.

"I tried to sleep in a shed attached to the house," Nichols wrote.

> *The "snuggins" as the quilts were called had never been washed and the odor did not smell like roses. They had eight children, and she had never had a doctor during her confinement. His* [the cowboy's] *mother took the place of the doctor. For food we had biscuits, golden yellow filled with soda. Fat meat swimming in grease with flies mixed in, and molasses with flies. I collected $60 and went back to Slaton.*

Nichols never revealed whether the twins survived.

A few days later, Nichols's father arrived in Slaton for a visit. He told his father, "I had had a belly full of general practice and wanted to go to New York and specialize in eye, ear, nose and throat." Nichols received a loan from the bank for the $1,200 it would cost him to stay six months in New York for his training.

"We boarded the train, reached New York, and took a horse-drawn carriage to a house on River Side Drive," Nichols wrote. That night, at the beer garden, Nichols retold his stories of West Texas, cowboy medicine and the new town of Slaton.

"We had talked to a woman in Lubbock whose sister lived in New York and rented apartments for $1 per day," Nichols wrote.

> *That night she took us to a beer garden where we heard Alexander's Ragtime Band. The next night the landlady had a poker game going on in the next apartment, and we decided to move out. We got a nice apartment in a new building near Columbia University for $5 a week. That night, we saw Broadway that we* [had] *heard about.*

The Pember Family, 1915

The same railroads that brought many to Slaton in 1911 brought a young Bruce Pember and his brother, Royce, with their mother, Lillian, from Iowa on September 15, 1915.

In the book *Slaton's Story*, Pember wrote about a long concrete sidewalk leading him for several blocks into the young town. In the distance, buildings lined Texas Avenue.

"I remember walking from the depot down a street with no improvements other than concrete sidewalks for several blocks," Bruce wrote. "Finally across the street there appeared a brick building of unusual shape." Bruce later learned that this was the location of the newspaper office and publishing house.

The family walked until turning a corner onto Garza Street.

"I looked to my right," Bruce wrote, "and saw a bucking horse and rider appear from behind a [different] brick building on Garza Street going north." The triangular structure Bruce refers to is the current chamber of commerce building on the corner of Garza and Panhandle. "The rider appeared to me for only a short distance. I remember that I felt I had surely come to a wonderful town."

The family made their way around the block, past confectionary stores such as Webb Confectionary, C.H. Fawcett Confectionary and Moore Confectionary, which were located on the 100 block of Texas Avenue. There was also a café located on 102 Texas Avenue. The Cozy Moving Picture Theater, the first theater and a modern luxury for any town at the

Two young boys work diligently at the Slaton Livery Barn, which was located on present-day West Panhandle Street on the Slaton Town Square, circa 1912. *Photo from* Slaton's Story.

Slaton Athletics have always been a dynamic part of the town. Pictured is the first Slaton High School girls' basketball team in 1915. *Photo from the Slaton Town Square Antique Mall and Museum.*

time, was on the corner of Garza and Ninth Streets. The theater building still stands today, anchoring the corner of Texas Avenue across the street from Citizens Bank. Before the family arrived at the hotel, they passed Howerton's Hardware and Undertaking on 160 East Lynn Street, Slaton's first funeral home.

On the night of their arrival, the family stayed at the Capps Hotel, a building that stands on the corner of Texas Avenue and Lynn Street. The red brick building is now in need of renovations but maintains its reminiscent exterior of the old hotel front, which once welcomed early visitors and the first residents of Slaton. In 1915, however, it was a modern hotel with fresh amenities, but it had trouble keeping the mosquitoes at bay because of the heavy rains that had fallen across the South Plains during the first years of Slaton's existence.

"Our first night was spent in a room on the second floor of the Capps Hotel," Bruce wrote. "It is most memorable as the night the mosquitoes nearly ate us up. So the next day, we moved to the Singleton Hotel."

Located on the corner of Ninth and Lubbock Streets, where Caprock Pharmacy is now located, the Singleton Hotel was the most luxurious hotel in Slaton in 1915. The hotel was later bought and became the Forrest Hotel in 1923. The hotel entertained and housed guests for decades before succumbing to a fire in 1953.

However, in 1915, Bruce, along with his mother and brother, went to eat in the dining room of this new hotel. "The waitress came to take our orders and mother ordered for all of us," Bruce wrote. "When the ordering was completed the waitress asked mother, 'do y'all want coffee?'"

"Oh, no the boys don't drink coffee," Lillian said.

"I mean you, yourself," the waitress replied rather haughtily.

A typical day in the 1920s on the Slaton Town Square. *Photo from the Slaton Town Square Antique Mall and Museum.*

"This first day or so taught us that we were a little different and had some adjusting to do," Bruce wrote.

The family eventually moved from the hotel and lived in a home at 905 South Twelfth Street.

Bruce would meet many other school-age children who would become his friends; of course, there were those few who didn't trust a "Northerner."

Bruce wrote that Bill Sledge and brothers Melvin and Victor Cade were often starting fights with him. It wasn't until years later when Bruce received a letter from Bill, who was in the army and stationed in Hawaii, that he was told about their hatred for him.

"I guess you have wondered why we picked a fight with you whenever our paths crossed?" Sledge wrote. "Victor did the fighting because Melvin and I were older and Vic was more your size but we thought of you as our enemy because you came from the North."

Bruce wrote that the letter went on to explain that since Sledge had been in the army, getting around in the world, he eventually learned that issues involving the "North v. South" were beginning to die prior to the 1920s.

When Bruce Pember's father, Merritt, first arrived in Slaton in 1914, he said the land was lush and the prairies were green from the rain. However, when he moved his family to Slaton, the rains stopped, and he faced a drought lasting until 1919.

Merritt's quest to Slaton had not been easy to begin with. He worked for Pember Hide and Fur House, buying furs from various parts of the world in Onawa, Iowa. When the fur market fell, he was forced to sell his stock of skunk furs.

While in Slaton, Merritt took on various ventures in agriculture and real estate and even shipped cattle bones out of Wilson. According to his granddaughters, Joyce Cheatham and May Belle Kern, Merritt also bought a Hart Parr tractor that pulled sixteen discs for a twelve-foot-wide cut and contracted breaking out land. When the tractor broke, he sent it to St. Louis, where a mechanic repaired the machine. It is believed, by some, that this was the first tractor in the area.

"He started broke," the Pember family wrote. "He gave checks for first day's purchases, took the goods to Lubbock, sold them and got the money to the bank in time to make the checks good."

It took Merritt five months to save $1,500. He worked as a real estate agent for a few years before buying a small insurance agency from C.C. Hoffman in 1919.

Soon after the trains came to Slaton, commerce flourished in the early 1900s. Here, gentlemen sit in front of the Slaton Cleaning Works, circa 1914. *Photo from* The Slatonite *archive.*

When Merritt bought the agency, the family was living in various rental houses throughout Slaton and even on a farm south of Slaton until they eventually settled in a house on 1025 West Garza Street.

In *Slaton's Story*, Bruce wrote, "We weathered the big blizzard that hit in January 1918 or 1919, but barely. All our cattle and others' drifted south until they hit a fence and then froze to death." Bruce wrote of snowdrifts several feet deep.

It was also during the winter of 1918 when several pioneering Slatonites lost their lives due to a flu pandemic that was sweeping the nation. "Dad caught the flu," Bruce wrote, "and we came very close to losing him."

Between 1919 and 1928, according to Cheatham and Kern, Merritt was a fairly successful businessman. The 1929 Depression, however, hit hard, and he lost his equities in five farms and eight rent houses.

Through hardships, difficulties and tragedies, the family continued to persevere, and Pember Insurance Agency remained a successful business for many decades.

Annie Schuette's Story, 2010

In 1916, a train pulled into Slaton, bringing in eight-year-old Annie Ehler and her family. A few days later, her father arrived by covered wagon.

Annie Ehler Schuette was born in Shiner, Texas, on October 22, 1909.

"How do I start," she said from her room at the Slaton Care Center that looks out onto the eighty-year-old Mercy Center Building she once watched being built. "It was very cold. There was a lot of snow," she said of her first memory of Slaton.

After her father sold their farm in South Texas, the young family of six siblings found their way to Slaton for better land opportunities. "A family friend told us about Slaton," she said. "They let us stay on their land when we first got here."

Schuette said the town was developing, and not very many homes had been built. She also said that most of the businesses were small wooden structures. "Our parents moved bedsprings on top of the corn," she said. This is where they slept in a small barn while their house was in the process of being built.

This same year, World War I raged overseas and affected Slaton during the town's infancy. "It was hard to find food at the time," Schuette said. "But our mother was a very good provider. We never went hungry."

During the relentless winter of 1916 that ensued, the family could not finish building their home until the weather subsided. "There was also only one contractor in town," Schuette said, "and since the Santa Fe Railroad continued to expand, he was busy building homes for all of the railroad people that were coming to Slaton."

Schuette said that after the war, Slaton really prospered. "We had plenty of food after the war," she said. "We didn't have to worry so much about losing any of it."

Instead of via school bus, Schuette traveled to school by horse and buggy. She attended school with her older sister and two neighbor boys, whom she said "protected us and treated us real good."

Two weeks into high school, Schuette said she developed an illness, preventing her from returning. She eventually went to work on the family farm. "There were very few of us that did finish," she said. "A lot of us stayed at home and worked on the farm because we had to work the fields. There was no one else to help us."

Schuette said many of the other families who lived on farms gathered every Sunday, "just to be together. Everyone brought food and we had a big luncheon. Everyone had a great time because there was so much open space."

When Schuette met her husband, H.G. Schuette, and moved into town in 1940, she became a stay-at-home mom while her husband ran a grocery store located near the former Slaton Lumber Company. H.G. later operated a service station and auto parts store. He passed away on December 6, 1975.

Annie Schuette celebrated her 100th birthday among family and friends at the Slaton Club House in 2010. The celebration was hosted by her children,

The desolate downtown streets of Slaton, circa 1919. *Photo from the Alton Kenney collection.*

daughters Amy Dubose, Mary Lee Schuette, Jonita (and Tim) Travland, Donita (and David) Kitten, Diana (and Ron) Sumner and son, Terry (and Deneice) Schuette.

Schuette also has twenty-four grandchildren, forty-three great-grandchildren and thirty-six great-great-grandchildren.

As long as her life may seem to some, she said she remembers her childhood days with fondness. "We played outside a lot then," she said. "We trusted each other and spent so much time playing baseball and walking the railroads."

She said one of her most fearful moments was when she first saw a plane fly over Slaton. "It was real low," she said. "It was so low my father thought it was going to hit us. He told us to get down on the ground, but we were too caught up in watching it fly over us. It was amazing."

As she looked out her window onto the town she saw grow, she said, "I just take things one day at a time. I've lived a day at a time because that's the only way you can live. You'll see…you just may be here someday."

The Flip of a Switch, 1920

On July 4, 1920, what began as a small flicker in a house on Railroad Avenue ignited a new generation. It ushered in a novel decade, bringing with it cultural shifts, changing mores and modern challenges and propelling citizens into the "decade of decadence."

With one twenty-five-horsepower Fairbanks Morse engine shipped via the Santa Fe Railroad, Slaton leapt out of the darkness when the Slaton Power Plant opened.

The Roaring Twenties had come to Slaton.

The Elliot family watched as an electric lamp illuminated their home. That same day, in approximately one hundred other houses across town, oil lamps burned out; electric bulbs took their place. Of course, electric service was only offered from dusk until midnight.

Slaton was never the same.

These were the years of Prohibition and flapper dresses, when the world's first ocean liners took to the seas and aeroplanes took to the skies and when Henry Dixon Loes wrote the children's gospel hymn "This Little Light of Mine," a song that later became an anthem for the civil rights movement.

Prior to electricity in homes, select businesses, such as movie theaters, had electricity produced by low-voltage generators. Electricity in households was a new development, even in large cities, and many families had apprehension about such a strong surge of power entering their homes. It had only been twenty-four years since George Westinghouse introduced the public to the Westinghouse Electric Company in 1895 in Buffalo, New York.

It is believed that the Slaton Power Plant was located in this building in the 1920s and was operated by James Elliot. *Photo from* Slaton's Story.

In 1921, fifty more Slaton families introduced electricity into their homes. This same year, the Hodge family decided that Slaton would become their new dwelling after leaving their hometown in Montgomery County, Texas.

"Not many black families were here, only about a dozen black children," Dora F. Johnson Hodge wrote in the book *Slaton's Story*. "At the time, though, farm work was like a gold rush in Slaton."

Also taking advantage of this "gold rush" and prosperity were Jesse Herman and Verna Dale Brewer, who moved to Slaton in 1915 from Duncan, Oklahoma. Jesse, who went by J.H., was the first president of the First State Bank.

The 1920s proved to be a prosperous time for the Brewer family, who built their home on 410 West Garza Street. The home became the site of various social gatherings and parties, bringing in the social elite of Slaton.

The Brewers became one of the most influential families in the 1920s. Verna was president of the PTA and highly involved in the Civic and Culture Club. J.H. was the director of the chamber of commerce and president of the Rotary Club and was named the Democratic Party precinct chairman.

On many nights, various people gathered at the Brewer home for their very popular, but exclusive, Bridge Club.

James Arthur Elliot, the man who brought electricity into the Brewer household, was acquainted with the Brewers. Elliot's wife, Sarah Callhan Elliot, was also a member of the Civic and Culture Club.

After Mr. Elliot's discharge from service following World War I, he came to Slaton to organize the Slaton Power and Light Company. The engine used generated only enough electricity to be offered in homes during the evening hours, "from dusk until midnight," as written in *Slaton's Story*.

The next year, as the Brewer family's social status in the community grew and the Hodge family continued struggling, *Slaton's Story* reported that "another engine of the same type and about fifty more customers were added and the plant operated one-half day each week for ironing to be done before 4:00 pm."

As electricity grew in popularity throughout Slaton, including in the Brewer household, the Bridge Club parties and gatherings became more popular. From the back of the Brewer home, the Hodge family could hear all that took place in the lighted Brewer household.

"It was a lonesome place," Dora F. Johnson Hodge wrote. "We lived in the servants' quarters in the back of the Brewer home." However, the Hodge family didn't stay long and moved to a location near the Santa Fe Reading Room. "We lived in a box car that had two rooms," Mrs. Hodge wrote. This was in 1923.

That same year, the Texas-New Mexico Utilities Company purchased the plant from James Elliot and offered twenty-four-hour service. *Slaton's Story* stated, "It was known as the Texas Utilities Company. A highline was built from the company's plant in Lubbock east of the Santa Fe tracks to Slaton."

On the outside, as technology advanced, Slaton grew, and the future seemed vibrant and illuminating. During this time, the community gathered in camaraderie as children sang, "Let it shine, shine, shine…Let it shine," completely unaware of the challenges this new decade in Slaton would bring.

Slaton Auto and Supply Company, circa 1915. *Photo from the Alton Kenney collection.*

Early Church Struggles, 1921

Two young boys, possibly wearing long white shirts buttoned up to the top and heavy gray trousers made of twill, very common in the 1920s, sat outside the Capps Hotel on the Slaton Town Square and watched as the people celebrated one unpleasantly bitter November night.

"I well remember the night of November 11, 1918," John Emmett Waldrop wrote in *Slaton's Story*, "when we received news that the Armistice ending the war was signed."

Waldrop and his friend Doc Castleberry watched in wonder and confusion.

"People all over town were firing guns into the air," Waldrop wrote. "We could hear buck shots rolling off the tin roof of the hotel. Loud explosions were coming from Mayben's Blacksmith Shop which was located where the fire station is now."

The two boys scurried from the Capps Hotel and made their way toward the ruckus at the blacksmith shop. "When we asked what was causing all the racket," Waldrop wrote, "we were told, 'They're shooting off anvils.' It took quite a while for two little boys to figure that out."

The First Baptist Church in Slaton, shown here about 1922, boasted a dynamic and thriving congregation throughout the '20s. *Photo from* Slaton's Story.

Throughout the nation, a hatred for Germans and those of German descent reached an all-time high. Even in Slaton, various newspaper articles in *The Slatonite* referred to Germans as "Barbarians and Huns."

This same year, the First Baptist Church slowly grew, but not without tribulations.

According to the book *Pioneer Preacher of the Plains* by John Peddigrew Hardesty, in the early 1920s the First Baptist Church was a congregation divided. "Pastors would try to get matters to run smoothly but soon would give up in disgust and defeat," Hardesty wrote.

In 1921, Hardesty was asked by Walter L. Tubbs, a general missionary under the State Baptist Convention, to serve in Slaton.

"I did not want to go to Slaton," Hardesty wrote. "Out of courtesy to the church I agreed to visit them and give my answer." Of course, even after visiting, Hardesty continued having his doubts, especially during one particular, emotion-filled meeting: "The deacons had quarreled, and one of them attacked another with an upraised chair during a deacons' meeting."

In a different part of town, according to *Slaton's Story*, Father Joseph Reisdorff of the St. Joseph Parish dealt with an influx of German families who had migrated to Slaton via the Santa Fe Railroad, which hired many and attracted them to town with the donation and building of the first Catholic church in Slaton. However, by 1919, a new building was needed to accommodate the inflowing families. The Catholic Church itself began in 1911.

Because of the new congregants, however, in 1920 the church was in dire need of a new building. By 1922, a parochial school had already been implemented for a year and was led by the Sisters of Mercy.

At the First Baptist Church, to help stabilize the troubled parish, Hardesty agreed to move out of his comfortable and stable town of Lockney and make his way to Slaton.

"I gave several reasons why I should not accept the call," Hardesty wrote. The first reason was that his family was accustomed to a lifestyle that kept them well fed and nicely clothed. The congregation matched his Lockney salary. The second reason was that the living quarters in Slaton were not up to his standards. The congregation gathered one afternoon to repaint and remodel the pastor's home. His third and final reason was that the move itself would be too expensive and untimely for the family. So residents of Slaton gathered trucks and moving supplies and made their

The Catholic Parsonage in the 1920s. *Photo from* Slaton's Story.

way to Lockney to move the family. "And that was that," Hardesty wrote. "Every objection I had raised was promptly met and remedied. What else could I say but yes."

Upon arrival, in 1921, Hardesty replaced the deacons of the church, and the congregation soon united. Before long, the church, like the St. Joseph Parish, had space problems, and they, too, began to look at constructing a larger place of worship.

However, across the way, in an entirely different town—perhaps because minorities were not permitted in various parts of Slaton—a group of people also had the urge to convene in solidarity, faith and spirit.

On the second Sunday of March 1921, under the direction of Deacon Aren Johnson, four African American families came together. The families of Arthur Jones, Reuben Johnson, Willie Bryant and Oscar Wilborn Sr. and the deacon peacefully met for the first time beneath a donated tent to praise and worship, just like the majority of the community of Slaton did every Sunday. This was the first meeting of the Mt. Olive Baptist Church.

In 1922, however, the First Baptist Church faced a new ordeal.

"One night a group of robed men quietly walked down the aisle of the church and the leader handed me a letter," Hardesty wrote.

> *I was commended for my stand on law and order, and the letter informed me that the Ku Klux Klan stood ready to aid all the forces for good in the community. Then they just as quietly filed out through the other aisle. Not a word was spoken and everyone sat in complete silence during the episode.*

CROSSBONES AND CANDY SHOPS, 1922

It was on the Slaton Town Square in 1922 that the familiar sweet smell of confectionery delights floated through the air as children made their way across town over dirt roads—or, if the rain had fallen within a few days' span, muddy streets—for sweet snacks and afternoon delicacies.

Having been on the square for six years, the J.H. Teague & Son, Confections, Drug, Sundries, was a local favorite.

The class of 1922 celebrates "Kids Day" at Slaton High School. *Photo from the Slaton Town Square Antique Mall and Museum.*

The Teague Candy Shop, seen here, was a popular hangout for youngsters throughout the 1920s. *Photo from* Slaton's Story.

By the early 1920s, the Teague family had built a successful business, and Joe Teague Sr. had already become a well-known citizen. Teague was such a successful businessman in Slaton that he became the first city marshal and later mayor (1939).

The Teague family began their business on June 15, 1911, the day thousands of people arrived in Slaton to start new lives in a new town developed by the Santa Fe Railroad. The Teague legend began when Joe Teague Sr. and Joe Teague Jr. worked for Hamlin Supply serving food to train crews. Five years later, in 1916, the two Joes opened their very own confectionery in the lobby of the Palace Theater. By 1921, they had developed a successful business on the town square and built twin houses for their families at 430 and 450 West Lubbock Street.

In the early 1920s, Slaton was a thriving city with a population of more than six thousand, and various candy shops and confectioneries fought and competed over satisfying Slaton's sweet tooth. The 1920s were a golden age for candy companies throughout the country, and some of the sweet treats still enjoyed today were introduced to the public during this savory era, including the Baby Ruth bar (1920), the Mounds chocolate bar (1923) and the Milky Way candy bar (1923).

Bonnie Abel Deering, as a young girl—possibly wearing heavy tweed outfits, Mary Jane shoes and thin white stockings, with lollipop breath and

Standing in front of a Dodge Roadster, Oran McWilliams, Andy Anderson, Jimmie Jean Moody and Bonnie Abel take a break at a filling station in 1920s Slaton. *Photo from* Slaton's Story.

chocolate-stained dresses—was no stranger to the Teagues' candy shop. "No one who ever lived in Slaton could possibly forget the Teague's Drug Store," she wrote in *Slaton's Story*. "Founded by old 'Uncle Joe Teague,' and later operated by his son, 'Little Joe Teague.' It was a sort of gathering place for the town's people at times, especially the young folk."

Deering wrote that there were various gatherings in the community during her childhood, but the most memorable were the church revivals.

"My father was a Baptist and my mother a Methodist so we attended both churches and had no problems," Deering wrote. "Most of the time we attended Sunday morning services at the Methodist and evening services at the Baptist."

Of course, in 1922, the Baptist Church continued with its social struggles. John Peddigrew Hardesty wrote:

> *I had been in Slaton exactly one year when I received the following letter:*
> *"July 4, 1922*
> *Lubbock, TX*
> *You are in for it. We attended several of your sermons in Slaton and the one here. We don't like your ideas. You are too much KKK and talk too much about other denominations. If you don't get out of this county in 10 days you will go out feet first. Try us and see.*

> *We do not go to church but we are too American.*
> *Skull and Crossbones"*

Hardesty received the letter a few weeks after the revival at the Methodist church. "In that meeting I had not hesitated to give sin a black eye," Hardesty wrote. "I had called a spade, a spade."

Hardesty wrote that immediately upon receipt of the letter, he went to the editor of *The Slatonite* and asked for space to announce his reaction. "I stated in the announcement that I would reply to the 'Skull and Crossbones' note in my sermon the following Sunday night," he wrote.

"How well I remember those revival meetings," Deering wrote in *Slaton's Story*.

> *They were usually held behind or at side of the buildings. Since there were no cooling systems in those days we had to sit outside or "burn up" or fan ourselves to death. We sat on hard benches made from new lumber and*

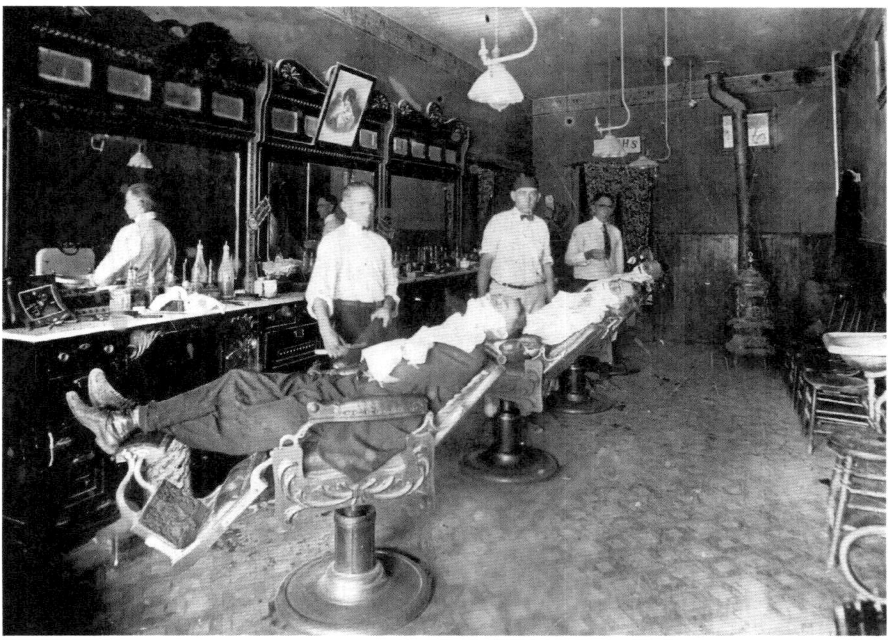

On Saturday afternoons, many men in Slaton frequented barbershops, such as the Joe Walker Sr. Barbershop seen here about 1922, to be cleaned up for Sunday church. *Photo from* Slaton's Story.

> *many people brought pillows. Bright, bare electrical bulbs were strung all around, and at night bugs for miles around went into orbit and came right there to do their dive-bombing. If the bugs didn't get you the mosquitoes did.*

Reverend Hardesty wrote that at that particular revival, on the night when he was to address the Skull and Crossbones militia, the Associated Press carried an account of it. "On Sunday night there were more people on the outside of the church building than on the inside," he wrote. "People came from a radius of fifty miles."

As the citizens uncomfortably sat and waited—some out of concern, some out of respect and some out of mere curiosity—Hardesty rose in front of the crowd and, "calmly and sweetly," gave his sermon. "I had come to Slaton in response to a united call of the church," he said before the anxious crowd.

> *I had not asked any one's permission to come, and I would leave Slaton just when I was good and ready to go; my family was enjoying the best of health and I knew of no good reason for a change; I was prepared to die; I liked Slaton, and had as soon be buried in Slaton as any place I knew.*

Soon after the revival, Hardesty wrote that the city council held a meeting in which it made him a "Special Officer" and told him that when he went out, especially at night, he should carry a gun.

Deering, who was a guileless child listening but not fully understanding the dangers, remembered the picnics, band concerts from the little band stand near the city hall, holiday parades, parties and dances in private homes. Through the sickly sweet scent wafting through Slaton streets from various confectioneries, she also remembered the revivals and had no true understanding, during her childhood, of the various workings of the Skull and Crossbones, the KKK or any other organization that, for decades before and after, blurred the line between miscreant and saint.

"We heard some wonderful preaching," she wrote, "and good singing, seems I can almost hear them now." She wrote that one of her favorite hymns sung at those revivals was "Shall we Gather at the River," and young Deering, wearing a short bob hairstyle, with small feet swinging beneath the pews, joined the chorus of people as they sang, "Soon we'll reach the silver river, soon our pilgrimage will cease; soon our happy hearts will quiver with the melody of peace."

The Tar and Feathering of Father Keller, 1922

On a Saturday night, March 4, 1922, what may have begun as a whisper, an aside, a comment or just mindless chatter amongst neighbors transformed the community and introduced an air of instability and perilous paranoia.

It was past the buds of bright red verbenas that the Civic Culture Club urged the people of Slaton to plant so visitors who passed through by train would come to know the town as, "Slaton—Home of the Red Verbena." It was beyond the altar that sat undisturbed in the dark church, already prepped for Sunday morning Mass in the St. Joseph Catholic Parsonage.

On that night, with only the light of the astonishing stars that have flickered against the skies from unknown regions throughout little-known histories, Father Joseph M. Keller staggered into the Slaton city limits, past cotton fields and newly built houses on the north end of town, verging on the appearance of a monster rather than a man.

Mostly nude, he limped, wearing nothing but a layer of tar and scorched skin, cooled only momentarily by the gentle night breeze, which, every once in a while, may have made some of the white feathers attached to his body flutter.

"He walked down the street that night," wrote John Peddigrew Hardesty in his book *Preachers of the Plains*, "with only one house shoe on, neither barefooted nor shod, to his room."

Father Keller may have screamed, he may have shouted or he may have cried out so loud that it would have shattered a thousand communion chalices.

The Catholic parsonage, seen here about 1917, welcomed many German Catholics to Slaton throughout the early settlement of the town. *Photo from* The Slatonite *archive.*

However, there are no known reports of anyone hearing anything unusual from the barren cotton fields. All that remains are the various accounts of what may have happened in that field and the years leading up to that one fateful night—nothing more than hearsay.

The murmurs and whispers had begun years before, in 1917, two years after the sinking of the *Lusitania* but the same year American troops fired the first shot in the trench warfare of World War I. That year in Slaton, anti-German sentiments radiated from *The Slatonite*, and Joseph M. Keller was chosen by the Catholic Diocese of Dallas to serve in the town after a brief stay in Hermleigh. His hometown, however, was thousands of miles away in Aachen, Germany.

The book *Slaton's Story* reported that the Catholic church in Slaton dates to the same year as the town's birth: 1911. The first Mass was held on December 8, 1911, on the day of the Feast of the Immaculate Conception, a Catholic holy day celebrating the Immaculate Conception of Mary. It was officiated by Father Reisdorff, with the two Catholic families of Frank Simnacher and A.L. Hoffman celebrating.

Because Father Reisdorff had an agreement with M.F. Klattenhoff that he would receive a commission on all land sold to the Catholic families who bought in the area, the church grew tremendously within four years, and by 1917, the time had come to appoint a new pastor. The new pastor was German native Reverend J.M. Keller.

J. Michael Carter of the Catholic Diocese of Amarillo wrote in an essay that when Keller arrived in the small town, chatter began early. "Keller's life entered a web of personality conflict and confusion," Carter wrote. "By this time, the First World War raged in Europe and the editor of the Slaton newspaper began to denounce the Germans as 'Barbarians and 'Huns.'" Carter also wrote that since Keller had strong feelings about the war, he eventually confronted the editor of *The Slatonite* with an "angry retort."

After this exchange, it is believed, the rumors began. "Soon the jaundiced eyes of Slaton turned toward Father Keller," Carter wrote.

The first rumor circulating was that the Kaiser, the emperor of Germany, whose policies helped bring about World War I, appointed several hundred priests to do spy work in the United States. Keller, at one point, was believed to have been one of those priests, especially since Keller insisted on keeping a picture of Kaiser Wilhelm above his desk and "did not remove it until his parishioners forced him to," Carter wrote.

When the United States entered the war, it is believed that Keller made a patriotic gesture at a rally by buying war bonds. The next week, at another patriotic rally, "the speaker had publicly denounced him because he was the only one who had failed to pay his share," Carter wrote.

The community was not pleased, and the congregation became more divided over Keller's appointment. According to Carter, "In 1918, some of the parishioners sent a petition to Bishop Lynch asking him to remove Father Keller but Lynch rejected the petition and ordered the petitioners to grant Keller the respect due him as a priest."

However, the people were not deterred, and the priest became a target for more personal ridicule and suspicion. Soon, Keller was accused of lechery and adultery by citizens, who also "claimed that he had syphilis," Carter wrote.

The complaints continued to the bishop, but once again, there was no hard evidence of suspicious behavior. "Bishop Lynch investigated these charges thoroughly," Carter wrote. "Documents of this investigation reveal that Keller was a man of odd habits and strange personality quirks, but no evidence could be found to support the more serious charges against him."

At this time, according to the book *Slaton's Story*, German families continued expanding the church's size and, in 1919, a third and larger church was built. This building, costing approximately $10,000, was finished in 1920 by the men of the parish.

Two years after the construction of the new building, the next round of rumors circulated. This time, the priest was accused of breaking the seal of confession and the people had had enough.

"On the night of March 4, 1922," Carter wrote. "Keller got up from his reading to answer a knock at the door."

When Keller answered the door, he was met by six masked men wielding pistols.

It is believed that one man fired a shot at the ceiling before the other men burst across the doorsteps and detained the shocked priest. Bound and gagged as the priest's terrified housekeeper watched, Keller was hauled away to a waiting car.

Carter wrote that Keller's assailants stuffed him down into the backseat and sped away, past the safety of the newly installed city lights and out into the dreadful darkness of the country night. "They drove out on a lonely road," Carter wrote. "To a place several miles north of town, and when they stopped, the terrified Keller rose up to see 15 or 20 men waiting for him."

Silence in Slaton, 1922

On Sunday, March 5, 1922, a meeting was held at the Odd Fellows Hall in Slaton. A statement was made to the Associated Press: "The citizens of Slaton gave approval and commendation to the act, and it is the unanimous conviction that a very undesirable citizen had been dispatched."

John Peddigrew Hardesty wrote in his autobiography, *Preachers of the Plains*. "There were some exciting times during those days, one night a group of men kidnapped the Catholic priest, took him to a secluded spot, whipped, tarred and feathered him."

The night before the meeting, however, many citizens hadn't known the extent of the attack or the brutality taking place beneath the stars.

Soon after the rumbling and rattling of the vehicle stopped, there may have been a brief moment of silence in the dark night. A small thought may have floated from man to man, but it was too late to go back. The decision had been made. Before the cruel and degrading tar and feathering, there was the lashing of whips slicing the air and cutting through Father Keller's skin.

After ripping off his clothes, it is believed that Father Keller's captors poured substantial blistering black tar over the priest before soft white feathers were thrown at him. As the tar cooled, encasing his skin and closing off his pores, the men left him out in the fields to find his way back.

Various accounts stated that the men told Keller, "You have twenty-four hours to get out of town," soon after the inhumane assault. There are no records of how long the beating lasted. All that is known is that Father Keller was left alone in the barren field of chirping crickets and crying coyotes. Facing no other options, Father Keller staggered back into town with one house shoe on, wearing an outfit of tar and feathers.

J. Michael Carter wrote in an essay for the Diocese of Amarillo:

> *The scourging ended after about 20 strokes, but the ordeal continued as the vigilantes proceeded to cover him with a coat of heated tar. Someone produced a pillow and after ripping it open, the group gleefully scattered feathers all over him.*

Hardesty claims that Dr. Tucker helped the priest in his time of crisis. "Dr. Tucker spent hours extracting the tar and feathers from his hide," he wrote. It is believed that Keller may have stayed with Dr. Tucker that night; however, the next morning he boarded a train at Posey "and left for parts unknown, he never returned to Slaton," Hardesty wrote.

Other documents show that Keller spent a few days healing in a hospital in Amarillo. Carter said that when Keller left Amarillo, he stayed in a St. Louis hospital, and it took him a year to fully recover from the incident—although some say he never truly did.

"Essentially, it would cause deep second- and third-degree burns," Michelle Harvey said in an interview in 2010. Harvey is a physical therapy supervisor for the University Medical Center in Lubbock and works regularly with burn victims. "Once the tar's been applied, you're talking about a risk of infection and a significant loss of fluids which can cause various problems, including organ failure and death." Harvey also said that since there were no regulations at the time concerning the temperature of tar, there is no accurate gauge of the extent of the trauma that may have been imposed on Keller.

Hardesty wrote that for months, "gum shoe men, and women, walked the streets of Slaton, trying to figure out, 'who done it,' but they had no luck."

Hardesty also wrote that the district judge stated he would "get to the bottom of this." However, nothing was ever done. "The public was too well satisfied."

Some have claimed that it may have been the work of the Ku Klux Klan; however, according to Hardesty, who neither acknowledged nor denied ever being affiliated with the Klan:

> *Certain ineligibles, men whose private life, or social and business connections were such as to bar them from membership, ganged together and pulled some rough stuff on a few hoodlums, and laid it to the work of the Ku Klux Klan.*

He added:

> *I did know a great deal about the work of the Klan in the early twenties. I do know that the law enforcement officers, school trustees, many of the county officials, including the sheriff, were Klansmen, and that the backbone of the evangelical churches of the community consisted of Klansmen.*
>
> *It is a fact, brought out in the open the next day, that at the very hour the priest was being tarred and feathered, a group of Catholic men were in the office of Attorney R.A. Baldwin, pleading with him to organize a, "party," to wait on the priest and do exactly what was at the moment happening to him* [Keller].

However, Carter wrote that the attack left many German Catholic residents in the community feeling apprehensive that they, too, could be attacked in their community. Even the Sisters of Mercy, who were in Slaton at the time, were advised to leave until mindsets were less hostile and the populace was, once again, forbearing.

Carter claimed that no Catholics were among the men who attacked Keller: "The attack provoked a response from Texas Catholics and several chapters of the Knights of Columbus sent letters to protest the City of Slaton." Carter also wrote that the National Catholic Welfare Council offered a $2,500 reward for information leading to the arrest and conviction of the guilty party. "Bishop Lynch watched and waited," Carter wrote. "He [Lynch] considered placing Slaton under interdict but soon he realized that the damage was done and the church [St. Joseph] would have to go on about its business."

Father Joseph Keller sits silently behind his home in Slaton, 1922. *Photo from the Amarillo Catholic Diocese.*

The whereabouts of Keller, however, did not remain a complete mystery. According to Carter and various historical documents, after his yearlong recuperation, Keller's last location was believed to be in Wisconsin.

According to a document about the history of St. Charles Borromeo Catholic Parish in Burlington, Wisconsin, on February 27, 1927, more than six thousand people attended the reception of a new reverend, Fredrick J. Hillenbrand.

"The time was spent in an informal manner," the document stated. "Music was furnished by Joseph Hoffman's Orchestra, which played from an alcove of banked ferns." It is believed that the Reverend Joseph M. Keller was one of the people who attended this party. He was serving at a parish in Brighton, Wisconsin.

With his scarred body and mind, Keller was surrounded by new camaraderie and a calm existence in Wisconsin. The murky night of March 4, 1922, as he was left to die in a bleak cotton pasture outside Slaton, remained a ghostly memory to him. One can only hope that the nightmare eventually wilted like the final petals of a red verbena in the beginnings of a Slaton autumn.

Keller died in 1939.

Movies in Slaton, 1920

May 19, 1910: doomsday.

On this day of gloom, many anticipated Earth's collision with Halley's Comet. Newspapers across the world announced that the earth would be brushing the tail of the comet in its orbit.

According to various sources, in preparation of the comet's arrival, telescope sales rose, and hotels offered special packages that included rooftop viewing of the possible catastrophic event.

The entire spectacle became nothing more than media hype when, on May 20, 1910, people awoke to the same planet Earth and the same workday. The panic left their minds, and they focused on the new hype: the silent moving picture theaters.

The next most-talked-about event of 1910 was the mass hit *Frankenstein*, a thirteen-minute-long silent film based on Mary Shelley's novel.

Nine years later, in 1919, Floyd Williams and Sam Selman opened the Wilselman Theater on the Slaton Town Square. Prior to this theater, the Cozy Moving Theater on the corner of Garza and Ninth Streets offered various silent films to the public. The Cozy was the first theater in town and was built sometime between 1911 and 1915.

However, the Wilselman Theater was the first major theater to have a sound system and could seat approximately 740 patrons during one showing. It was also the first theater that brought major blockbuster movies, such as *Broken Blossoms*, *Daddy Long Legs* and the number one hit of 1919, *The Miracle Man*.

Slaton's first movie theater, circa 1920. *Photo from the Slaton Town Square Antique Mall and Museum.*

In 1920, as dramas played out on screen, the drama also seeped into the business. The theater was, once again, sold—to Jeff Custer, who operated the venture through 1925. During this time, Slatonites were treated to films such as the *Mask of Zorro* (1920) staring Douglas Fairbanks Sr., and the lavish adventure film *Robin Hood* (1922).

There is little known about how many citizens of Slaton, or those passing through by train, enjoyed the theater. It is known, however, by many accounts, that the theater business in Slaton remained a powerful force for many decades.

In 1927, many renovations and modern advancements were added under the ownership of Oscar Korn. The theater also changed names and became known as the Palace Theater. Later, Walter Buenger became the owner.

A newspaper clipping published in the 1950s in *The Slatonite* read:

> *The theater has been under the management of several different managers but none of them has met with the success that Mr. Walter Buenger has in winning the favor of local citizens and establishing the good will of the theater generally through this territory.*

Mr. Walter Buenger was originally from Monahans. He spent two and a half years, prior to coming to Slaton, in Monahans and Tyler, where he learned the skills necessary to the successful operation of a show house.

The Custer Theater on the Slaton Town Square. *Photo from the Slaton Town Square and Antique Mall.*

For generations, many citizens of Slaton enjoyed the luxury of the modern movie theater and witnessed the industry's advance from silent double features lasting twenty minutes to major studio blockbusters.

Edna Walter's Story, 2010

In the early 1900s, it is believed that society advanced at a far greater pace than at any other time in history. Prior to the invention of radio and television, and only a few years after the invention of the automobile, the country was on the verge of facing difficulties, challenges, struggles and tragedies. It was during this time, on August 4, 1910, that Edna Walter was born in Shiner, Texas.

"You gotta be tough to get old," Walter often said. She would know. She lived through World War I, the Great Depression, World War II, Vietnam and all the post-9/11 struggles, to name a few.

Walter lived the first seven years of her life in Shiner before the family decided to move west, loading their belongings on a train. Their father, George Ehler, rode a horse and buggy, while Edna and her mother, Annie; sisters, Hattie, Velma, Nola; and brothers, Edwin and Herbert, drove a car and made their way to the Slaton area in 1917.

During the first couple of decades of the 1900s, it's easy to imagine Edna Walter in her favorite homemade purple dress, socializing and dancing. "Oh, there was lots of dancing," Walter said. "We danced quite a bit."

During her childhood, Walter remembered playing baseball, forty-two and other hand games. She said, however, that they didn't have much time to play because they spent most of their time working in the fields.

"I probably started picking some cotton at eight or nine," Walter said.

"That made them tough," Melvin Walter, Edna's son, said. "Working in the fields made them very tough."

Of course, the family's first few years in the Slaton area would be tougher than anticipated. Walter said they didn't have much success with their cotton crops during those years. "I know we had some big snowstorms," she said. She also said that the flu of 1918 affected most of her family.

One of the people who helped her family through the struggles, Dr. Sam Houston Adams, was the physician at the time in Slaton.

"He was a good man," Walter said. When Dr. Adams was murdered in 1932 at the hands of a father of one of his patients, Walter remembered the tragedy, which left a blemish on the history of Slaton. "I felt so sorry that happened," she said of the murder. "I felt so bad when I heard someone had shot him. He was a good man, a gentle man."

Walter also remembered the stock market crash of 1929, launching the Great Depression that lasted twelve years. "We lived on the farm and had our own food; [the Depression] didn't hurt us as much as people who didn't have gardens," she said. "All we bought during that time was coffee, sugar and flour. We only got enough to get by with. I had to use it sparingly, but we's was OK."

In 1933, after years of living on the farm, Edna and friends decided to load a vehicle and take back roads out of town, making their way to Chicago for the Century of Progress International Exposition, the World's Fair, one of the most elaborate and historical expositions in history.

"They had all kinds of things there," Walter said. "There were lots of things I had never seen."

In her mid-twenties, Edna attended the Lutheran church in Wilson, where she played in the orchestra and met her husband, Adolph Walter. At the age of twenty-seven, on November 17, 1937, she married Walter. He was thirty-five. The couple had three children, two boys and one girl; seven grandchildren; and eleven great-grandchildren. Both sons and all seven grandchildren attended and graduated from Lubbock-Roosevelt High School.

Edna and Adolph eventually moved to Lubbock, where, for three years, she ran a grocery store with a restaurant in the back with her aunt. She said that they sold hamburgers at the restaurant for the price of six cents for one burger or six burgers for a quarter.

In 1939, Walter and her husband moved into the house where she still resides outside Ransom Canyon. She remembered when soldiers practiced training in the cotton fields surrounding their house during World War II.

In 1925, the citizens of Slaton crowd around the town square gazebo in honor of San Jacinto Day. *Photo from* Slaton's Story.

She remembered watching her children, Doris, Melvin and James, play on the ice during the Great Ice Storm of 1949. She remembered using coal-burning lanterns before electricity lines were placed in the rural countryside in the 1950s. She also said that she had a lot of good times to remember.

But, most of all, she remembered being young and dancing. Dancing in her favorite purple dress.

The Dust Bowl Era, 1920s

It was the late 1920s, and all the rage among the young children was prairie dogs.

"There was a large area approximately six or eight blocks between the Tudor residence and the Ben White and Robert Shankle's residence," Ray Darwin wrote in *Slaton's Story*. "This area housed a huge Prairie Dog town, which provided a favorite playground for the children and a sport of 'trapping Prairie Dogs' in wooden boxes that had trap doors and then trying to tame them for pets."

For the older kids in town, the late 1920s was a grand era for Slaton Tiger football. In 1927, according to *Slaton's Story*, the school celebrated the Slaton Tigers' district championship win. That same year, they defeated Canyon for the bi-district honors.

The next year, in 1928, Mrs. R.L. Wicker organized the Slaton City Line Home Demonstration Club for the adults in town. "The purpose of this club was to improve living conditions in and around Slaton," as stated in *Slaton's Story*. "When the club was organized, one of the worst sandstorms ever was blowing," the article said. This was a precursor of the Dust Bowl that affected the Great Plains. Various accounts noted the terrible dust storms that plagued Slaton and the entire plains region of the United States and southern Canada during the late '20s and well into the '30s.

During the Dust Bowl era, "black blizzards" swept across the plains, and no Slatonite was spared from the darkened skies and painfully sharp dust shards that lashed homes, buildings, vehicles, animals and people.

One of the many monstrous dust storms that altered the livelihoods of Slatonites in the 1930s, at the height of the Dust Bowl era. *Photo from the Slaton Town Square and Antique Mall.*

"We could see it," longtime Slatonite Annie Schuette said of the dreadful dust storms that wreaked havoc on the still-growing town. "They were like dark clouds," she said. "Then black as night."

"They were scary sometimes," longtime Slaton resident Mary Enloe said of the storms in a 2010 interview. "My mother thought the world was coming to an end some days and, on some days, we believed her."

"I have many interesting and pleasant memories of my childhood in Slaton," Darwin wrote.

> *Having a horse and endowed with a roaming nature, I gave my parents many anxious moments, leaving by horseback at dawn, and not coming back until dark—riding over the wide open country and exploring every ravine—wash and hill in the canyon.*

Darwin's parents had reason to worry. Those years were the beginnings of darkening skies and the sweeping away of the plains as dust storms forced topsoil to travel far beyond West Texas, as far as the Atlantic coastline.

In its original state, Slaton—and a vast majority of the Great Plains—was covered with natural grass and shrubbery that held the soil in place. As the city grew and agriculture became an important addition to the railroad town, the topsoil became more exposed to the danger of erosion by the winds that frequently raged across the rolling plains.

Then, beginning in the early 1930s, a severe drought gripped the area.

According to the *Texas History Handbook*, in 1932 there were fourteen recorded dust storms. In 1933, the number of dust storms increased to thirty-eight. By 1936, the number of dust storms reached an astonishing sixty-eight, and throughout the decade, the frequency and severity of the storms continued to increase at remarkable and treacherous rates.

"Nothing would grow because we didn't have any rain," Schuette said. "It was just as black in front of your face as it was anywhere else." Schuette remembers one particular storm when she was forced to rush inside with her two young children and hide in the basement until it passed. "During that storm my husband was working in the fields," she said. "Because it was so dark, he couldn't find his way home."

"They would come in on a big roll," Enloe said. "We had to go in and the rest of the day was dark."

"We had to kill our cows," Schuette said. "We couldn't find any food to feed them because we just didn't have any rain."

"During the 1930s the depression was making farming almost impossible," Mary Grace Privett wrote in *Slaton's Story*. "Farm prices had sunk to a new low." According to Privett, her family had very successful crops in the early '20s. This financial gain helped the family purchase land east of Slaton in 1924. "I recall my father using a Ford tractor to break the sodded land that first year. He plowed all day and night and sometimes I would keep the tractor going while he ate," she wrote. "I remember being so proud, as an eight-year-old, to be able to help."

Privett wrote that she attended East Ward School in Slaton and graduated from primary school wearing the original school colors—purple and white capes and hats. Soon after Privett completed primary school, however, the family's struggles during the Depression and Dust Bowl era eventually turned into a daunting departure from a desolate farm for the family.

"Our departure from the farm began on Thanksgiving Day when a terrible sandstorm blew out the ungathered cotton," Privett wrote.

> *My father, who was coming home from the gin in an empty wide-bed wagon, sustained a broken hip when the bed was blown off the wagon by those same high winds. He lay for several hours near a playa lake in our pasture before he was found covered with mud.*

Suffering from sandblasted skin and bloodshot red eyes, and some people left to the point of near-starvation because of the storms and the ongoing recession, the early 1930s became a very trying and difficult time for most, including Schuette. "I measured everything so we wouldn't waste a spoonful, and that's how we made ends meet," Schuette said. "All we knew was to buy what we had to have. Most people today don't have a clue what it was like, but it was tough times. Very tough times."

However, Slatonites tried, as best they could, to survive the turbulent 1930s. On some days, as people waited for the storms to pass, many recalled the '20s and all the blessings they once had. For Ray Darwin, one of those recollections was about the prairie dogs they tried taming. "There were many fingers and hands pierced by their sharp teeth. The mothers disapproved of this pastime as the prairie dog town was also a favorite place for rattlesnakes; however, to my knowledge there was no fatality."

But of course, the 1920s became just that—only memories drifting through the consciousness of Slatonites like the lingering scent of rain.

Then Came 1929

In 1924, several people made their way to the Slaton City Hall and, over radio, listened as their young, hometown girls sang. For the first time, calming voices of Slatonites traveled far beyond the prairie lands.

"An outstanding event in my school life was in 1924," Julia Alice Florence Lane wrote in *Slaton's Story*. "Several of us girls played in the band and sang at the Fort Worth Stock Show." From the stock show, a live broadcast feed of the event was played over the radio. "The people of Slaton met at the City Hall to hear us over loud speakers."

Two years later, once the excitement of the Fort Worth Stock Show had subsided, in 1926 the town met again for the wedding of Muriel Tudor.

"I was born on August 6, 1911," Tudor wrote in *Slaton's Story*. "I had the honor to be the first girl to be born in Slaton." Tudor came from a long lineage of settlers, including her father, R.H. Tudor, who built some of the first houses in Slaton. She married Albert O. Smith, who was the manager of the Slaton Theater at the time.

That same year, Opal Mosley Walston was a young girl beginning her education at East Ward School. She was a young girl who often walked past Albert O. Smith and Muriel Tudor, as she enjoyed spending the weekends at the movie theater during her childhood.

"On Friday nights, each family that could spare twenty-five cents was at the movies," Walston wrote in *Slaton's Story*. "A whole family could attend for a quarter and usually a double feature and a comedy were shown."

Walston wrote that another event considered "great family entertainment" was when citizens went to the red depot and watched trains pass through. She wrote that in later years, special trains ran to and from Lamesa for the annual rival football game: "Almost the entire population of Slaton would attend. One time among the many games that Slaton High School won, the Lamesa fans were so angry they made us walk from the stadium to the depot in the snow."

During the final years of the 1920s, as electricity became common, streets were paved, more houses were built and even more cars traveled the roads (horses and buggies, like outhouses, were becoming rare sights in the late '20s), citizens read in *The Slatonite* that the economic forecast was becoming bleak as people borrowed from banks at a furious rate, with little to no money to pay them back.

Then came 1929.

In October 1929, the stock market crashed, and the grand decadence and luxurious lifestyles of the 1920s fell with it. The technological advancements that filled people's homes, the candy shops that lined the square and the accomplishments of the people of Slaton quickly lost their luster as the widespread fear of the troubled times ahead hung heavy on the citizens.

The Brewer house, home of J.H. Brewer, president of the First State Bank, once filled with grand parties and social activities, continued to be a social center for the majority of 1929 and the early '30s. However, the Brewers weren't completely spared from the economic catastrophe.

"J.H. was president of the First State Bank," Katrina Brewer McDavid wrote in *Slaton's Story*. "It was a position he held until the disastrous depression. The bank survived the first, 'run,' but its backers were unable to convert holdings to pay off customers the second time and the doors closed in 1932."

In a different part of town, in a different household, young Opal Mosley Walston and her family dealt with the hardships in a different manner. "During the depression years, my dad helped the farmers by letting them have groceries all year until their crops were gathered," Walston wrote. "In the fall our back yard was filled with bales of cotton that were used to pay those bills. Many of the town women paid with handmade quilts."

As the decade of self-indulgence quickly transformed into one of the most unforgiving times in history, on the southwest part of town a grand building was assembled. It was the most ambitious architectural structure raised in Slaton. Deep into the autumn season, when the lush prairie turned brown and the trees became bare, showing no sign of life, on an unseasonably warm autumn afternoon, the citizens of Slaton witnessed the opening of Mercy Hospital.

"New $125,000 Building Virtually Complete; One of the Finest Institutions in the Southwest" was the headline of *The Slatonite* on Friday, November 22, 1929.

Mercy Hospital 1929

Barks…

Then growls…

Then fangs…

A violent collision of blood, fur and deafening howls erupted one April afternoon in 1929, when two dogs, one belonging to the C.B. Beal family and the other to the A.R. Keys family, became knotted in a mesh of dog-enraged dominance.

On Wednesday, April 24, 1929, a telegram was sent to *The Slatonite* with the following message from Dr. S.W. Beal of Austin: "Positive evidence of Rabies. Report for treatment if inoculated."

The brutal dogfight solidified in Slatonites' minds what many people in the area already knew. Because of the substantial growth of the town, a hospital was necessary. The same week of the rabies outbreak, construction of Mercy Hospital began.

On Monday morning, April 22, 1929, steel beams rose from the lot of the new sanitarium. According to *The Slatonite*, the building was constructed by the Dallas-based company Brennan Construction Company. "Fred Koch of the Dallas office of the Brennan Construction Company is here in charge of the work as Superintendent," *The Slatonite* stated. "Joe Brennan of Amarillo, a member of the company holding the general building contract, was here Monday assisting Mr. Koch in getting the work started."

The construction of the building was estimated at a cost of $125,000. Adding in the price of equipment, the hospital cost was estimated at approximately $200,000. "The new building will be four stories, including basement, and will have dimensions of 37 by 116 feet," *The Slatonite* noted. "It will accommodate about 50 patients and will be equipped with all the latest hospital features, including X-Rays and other equipment necessary to make the institution rank as one of the best sanitariums in Texas."

According to the article, the Sisters of Mercy, with headquarters in Stanton, were in charge of owning and operating the hospital.

However, planning for the hospital began in 1928. Not truly knowing the hardships the Depression would impose on people, the citizens of Slaton took a giant leap of faith and invested in the expensive undertaking. The people opened their hearts and wallets in the name of faith and healing. According to *Slaton's Story*, "The citizens of Slaton were asked by Reverend T.D. O'Brien to donate two city blocks valued at $3,000 plus a cash bonus of $20,000."

In another article in *Slaton's Story*, the Altar Society of St. Joseph Catholic Church donated a substantial amount of money by fundraising and soliciting donations. According to *The Slatonite*, a large cash bonus was given by the people of Slaton and the surrounding community to secure the hospital's location. "The Slaton Chamber of Commerce conducted the campaign to raise and collect the funds," an article in the newspaper read. The city approved the land site between Nineteenth and Twentieth Streets, and the people met the financial obligations. In the April 26, 1929 edition of *The Slatonite*, the front-page headline read, "Work Started Here Monday on Hospital."

However, for the families involved in the dogfight, it was too late, and six victims of the incident drove to Austin for treatment. "Though no member of the Beal family had been bitten by the dog, they had come into contact with its blood following the fight," *The Slatonite* reported. "The dog, rubbing against Mr. Beal, had gotten blood on his trousers. He wiped it off with a cloth, it was said, and then Mrs. Beal used the same cloth and wiped her arm, which had scratches thereon."

The Beal family, including their "little son," Charles, made their way to Austin for rabies treatment. The article also stated that the twelve-year-old daughter of Mrs. A.R. Keys also made contact with one of the dogs and was driven to Austin by her parents for the Pasteur treatment.

However, in the rural countryside of Slaton, where Annie Schuette lived, life was calm and comfortable. "1929 was a pretty good year," Schuette said. "We had a nice looking Model-T Ford and a good house to live in."

On the Wednesday afternoon of November 27, 1929, the citizens of Slaton gathered in front of the immense hospital building that was to become a permanent fixture on the humble Slaton skyline. "The program will begin in the morning, continuing again in the afternoon, and visitors will be permitted to inspect the new building through the day," a November 22, 1929 article in *The Slatonite* stated.

"I remember when they had a celebration," Schuette said. She had given birth that year to her first child, a daughter named Amy. "I stayed in the parking lot with the baby," she recalled. "You couldn't find a parking place because there were so many people there."

The people watched as public officials led the joyous ceremony, and then the patrons made their way through the new hospital and gazed upon the sterile equipment that shimmered beneath the fresh hospital lights. "The institution will be one of the finest and most complete in the Southwest," *The Slatonite* read. "Literally hundreds of people from all parts of the South Plains region are expected to attend the ceremony."

Schuette, a proud young mother at the age of twenty when she attended the formal opening, said what she remembered most was the sight of her newborn baby lying on the front seat of the car, away from the great crowd.

"She had a pretty little hat on," Schuette said. "She looked so pretty. That was eighty years ago, and I still remember what she looked like. She was so beautiful. Everyone would walk by and say, 'What a pretty little baby—what a pretty little baby.'"

Schuette, who was born in 1909 and celebrated her 101st birthday in October 2010, said they had no inclination of what the magnitude of the

Mercy Hospital, built in 1929, today is a thriving Catholic retreat center. *Photo from Mercy Center.*

stock market crash of 1929, one month prior to the opening ceremony of the Mercy Hospital, would be. The citizens of the town also had no foresight of the dust storms that would sweep across the Great Plains and ravage the once-fertile lands. In 1929, life went on as usual. "We had no way of knowing what was going to happen," Schuette said of the devastating 1930s.

Schuette and the community took in the festivities completely unaware that it was the beginning of a decade that would clamp down on the community of Slaton, and most of humanity, like a mad, rabid dog.

A Tale of Two Railroad Cities, 1927

In August 1911, Slaton was a lush, green prairieland following the heavy spring rains of that year. For the first year of the city's existence, the talk of the town was the proposed $75,000 plan to build the Harvey House.

"Does this look like temporary building, oh 'ye knockers?" the *Slaton Journal* asked on August 10, 1911. "Slaton is destined to become the leading city of this great railroad line."

"As may be expected, the locating of the Santa Fe division point at Slaton instigated bitter rivalry between Slaton and Lubbock," Reverend Lowell C. Green wrote in an article for *The Slatonite* in 1953.

"The town was taking on the aspects of a well built and orderly little city—bricks were replacing the first wooden affairs," Vyola Hubbard noted in *Slaton's Story*.

As the city grew, so too did the rivalry. A headline in the *Lubbock Avalanche-Journal* on March 28, 1912, read, "Lubbock is the Railroad Center of this Section."

"Appended was a map showing various small towns of minor significance," Green wrote. "Slaton was not even indicated on the map."

"There was a standing feud between Lubbock and Slaton all the way from politics to football," Hubbard noted. "We girls felt like that the boys who dated the Lubbock girls were super traitors, but when the situation went into reverse, somehow there was a difference."

In June 1912, Slaton, in an olive branch gesture by letter, sent to the citizens of Lubbock, stated:

The Slaton Santa Fe Depot in the 1920s. *Photo from the Slaton Town Square Antique Mall and Museum.*

> *We, the Commercial Club members and citizens of Slaton, invite you to participate in our celebration and development anniversary of June 14–15 with the view that your city be well represented and that a more binding and friendly feeling be established between Lubbock and Slaton.*

"Across the world, which was far-far away in those days, Europe was blowing itself to bits along with a lot of kings and emperors and rich ruling classes—I seldom thought of it being too recent a student of the American Revolution to care what happened to England," Hubbard wrote of the first World War. "I remember thinking that Germany would push that little island off the map—and then maybe she would come over and do something about Lubbock—prophesying was never one of my strong points."

As the area grew, so did opportunity. Various documents and oral histories indicated that Slaton was one of the proposed sites for the largest comprehensive higher education institution in the western two-thirds of the state of Texas. Lubbock eventually won the bid from the State of Texas, and Texas Technological College opened its doors in 1925 with an enrollment of 914.

On June 10, 1955, Slaton's first diesel train pulls into the Slaton Depot. *Photo from* The Slatonite *archives.*

"Texas Tech was supposed to be in Slaton," longtime Slaton resident the late Cecil Scott said in an interview in *The Slatonite* in 2008. "The people of Lubbock promised to build the university between Slaton and Lubbock so both cities could benefit from it, but that never happened."

What did happen, however, was that in 1925, Lubbock High School fell to the Slaton Tigers in the final game of the football season. It was also decided later that school year that the road to Lubbock would be paved, prompting various reactions throughout the community.

"I remember also the day my father, who was county commissioner, signed the contract to hard surface the road between Slaton and Lubbock," Hubbard wrote. "He looked so dejected."

"I gave Slaton a body blow today," Hubbard's father, H.D. Talley, said with a sigh.

"But daddy, that road is for Slaton too," Hubbard protested.

"You'll see," Talley replied.

The road was paved in April 1927.

Love in the Time of Influenza, 1932

The murder of Dr. Sam Houston Adams is not a tragic tale. It's not necessarily a gloomy story. Nor is it a hopeful story about overcoming hardships or tribulations. It's not quite folklore either. No, for lack of a better description, it is simply a love story.

It's a tale of love shared between two people, their daughters and the place they called home—Slaton. It is a love story beginning in 1918, the year of the influenza.

Like most of the world in 1918, Slaton was not completely spared by the flu epidemic. However, according to some, it may have been rescued from the worst of the flu's deathly grip through the tireless efforts of one of its citizens.

As most townspeople stayed in their homes, seeking shelter from the monstrous blizzards during the winter of 1918, on any given day, Dr. Sam Houston Adams was seen roaming the wintry streets. "Many developed the dreaded pneumonia, which was the real killer, more than the flu. Dr. Adams often brought in wood and built fires, fixed food, and administered to the sick in any way necessary," Dr. Adams's daughters, Frances Adams Kerrigan and Josephine Scott Adams Westefeld, wrote in *Slaton's Story*. "He slept with his clothes on for eleven days, and though his entire family had the flu at the same time, he never got sick."

Whether it was late into the hours of night or early in the morning, through sleet and snow, carrying his doctor's bag, going on little to no sleep and with calomel and castor oil on hand, Dr. Adams traveled from house to house, treating citizens affected by the deadliest pandemic since the bubonic plague.

Dr. Sam Houston Adams, one of Slaton's most well-respected citizens, was tragically murdered in his office on the Slaton Town Square in 1932. *Photo from the Slaton Town Square Antique Mall and Museum.*

"Besides the big snow of 1918, the great influenza epidemic caused the deaths of millions of people in the country and throughout the world," Frances and Josephine Scott wrote. "The little community of Slaton had at least one member in every household with the disease, and often a whole family was stricken at one time."

After he aided those who had been stricken by the influenza, it was his wife, Julia Ann Adams, who consoled the doctor and supported him that demanding winter.

According to *Slaton's Story*, the Adamses met years before, never suspecting they would be spending the rest of their days in a town that did not yet exist. It was the summer of 1905, and young Dr. Adams looked across a crowded room at a church meeting in Plainview, Texas, to see the love of his life, Julia Ann. "He saw a young lady at a church meeting," Frances and Josephine Scott wrote. "On asking his friend who she was, he said, 'I'm going to marry her.'"

More than a year later, on Christmas Eve, Julia Ann Price agreed to become Mrs. Adams. The couple was married on October 1, 1907, in Plainview. They lived in Louisville for two years as Dr. Adams completed medical school.

In 1911, the Atchison, Topeka and Santa Fe Railroad appointed Dr. Adams as the local surgeon for a new town being developed fifteen miles south of Lubbock. By train, the young couple made their way to the new frontier town with a briery name—Slaton.

"For several years, Dr. Adams was the only physician in Slaton, and he and Mrs. Adams underwent the hardships of the usual lot of pioneer families in a new country," Frances and Josephine Scott wrote. For many years he walked to make his calls in the town. Across from his office, where vacant buildings now stand on West Panhandle Street, a once-thriving livery stable stood. From the stable, he would hire a horse and buggy for rural calls.

In 1915, the Adamses built a house at 255 South Tenth Street. Almost unchanged, the house continues to modestly stand on a street corner.

Children play at the home of Dr. Sam Houston Adams. *Photo from the Slaton Town Square Antique Mall and Museum.*

Many of the organizations and civic duties the Adamses overtook also continue to flourish. They were the driving force behind building the first Methodist church. Although Dr. Adams was reared as a Baptist, he converted to the Methodist faith when he married the love of his life, who happened to be Methodist.

Another institution the Adamses assisted in establishing was Slaton's first school. Prior to the building of Slaton schools, classes were held at the Methodist church. When the new school was built, coal stoves were used to keep the children warm. "Dr. Adams went many a morning, before school, to build the fires," Frances and Josephine Scott wrote. "He served many years as a member of the school board and twelve years as its chairman."

In 1923, as other doctors moved into Slaton, Dr. Adams and his family of four loaded their vehicle and went on their first vacation since moving to the town. At the time, the family consisted of the couple and their two daughters. "Little Josephine's grandfather, Winfield Scott Adams, was so disappointed when their second child was a girl, that they named her Scott for him," Frances wrote.

Before the school buildings were erected, from 1911 to 1913, classes were held for the children of the town at the Methodist church. *Photo from the Slaton Town Square Antique Mall and Museum.*

It is believed, based on accounts in *Slaton's Story*, that this adventure was a pleasant and joyous event in the young family's life. It had been thirty-seven years since Dr. Adams had visited his birthplace near Lumpkin, Georgia. "The house he was born in had long since burned, and only a brick chimney with a crepe myrtle brush remained," Frances and Josephine Scott wrote. "We visited many historical places and returned to Georgia other times, but it was never so great an adventure as in 1923."

Throughout the 1920s, the family continued thriving, and in 1925, the Adamses' first daughter, Frances, set out to make a life of her own when she enrolled in Texas Women's College in Fort Worth. It was five years later, in 1930, when their youngest daughter, Josephine Scott, followed in her sister's footsteps. Frances eventually transferred to the University of Texas before finding her niche in the dramatic arts and made her way to New York City, where she enrolled at the American Academy of Dramatic Arts.

In August 1932, as the Adamses' daughters continued on their ventures of establishing lives outside Slaton, Woodie Tudor, son of R.L. Tudor, who built many of the first Slaton homes, was involved in an auto accident in which he sustained a broken arm. When his father took him to see Dr. Adams, it is believed that R.L. told Dr. Adams that Woodie had a weak heart, and he should avoid ether. However, the mistake had already been made—ether had already been administered.

Forty-five minutes after the mix-up, Woodie died.

It was two months later, on October 13, 1932, that Julia Ann discovered her husband's body, surrounded by a shallow pool of blood, lying lifeless on the cold floor of his office on Ninth Street, where a dry cleaning business now stands.

Dr. Sam Houston Adams was fifty-eight years old when he was shot with a revolver held by another grieving Slaton father, homebuilder R.L. Tudor.

CRIME OF THE CENTURY

The land continued baking in the hot sun. The ground's topsoil had withered down to a concrete-like substance of clay earth. The wind maintained its dry-heaving howls, and in 1932, rain was a rare occurrence in Slaton. As was murder.

It was not the familiar sounds of train whistles that cut through the azure West Texas skies on the Tuesday afternoon of October 13; rather, it was the sharp thuds of gunshots ricocheting across the cordial Slaton Town Square, according to a 1932 article in the *Lubbock Avalanche-Journal* that reported the trial of murder suspect R.L. Tudor.

"Oh, please don't shoot," Dr. Sam Houston Adams begged.

Shots rang out multiple times, striking Dr. Adams in each arm and once in the abdomen.

"Please don't shoot me any more," Dr. Adams pleaded.

It was too late. The adored pioneer doctor quickly lost blood.

Moments later, J.W. Nesbitt, a close friend of Adams and Tudor, stood motionless on the sidewalk outside of the doctor's office. He saw Tudor walking toward him with a gun.

"My God, Lee, what did you do?" Mr. Nesbitt asked.

"He killed my boy and I shot him," Tudor stated.

Nesbitt later said, on cross-examination during the trial, that he saw children near the physician's office when he first heard the shots.

Across the street, Precinct Two constable Ragan Reed crossed the street at the sounds of what he described as "a car backfiring" and made his way to the doctor's office. He, too, saw the gun in Tudor's hand.

Outside, Reed said Sheriff Tom Abel approached Tudor.

"I killed Dr. Adams, I reckon. I tried to," Tudor told Abel.

"He [Tudor] hesitated a little then turned the gun over to Mr. Abel," Reed said in court.

Reed testified that he saw two little girls run away from near the front of the doctor's office. He said they appeared to be trying to look through the plate glass window of the office.

Reed then rushed into Dr. Adams's office to find Joe Stokes and F.J. Hilders aiding Dr. Adams to his feet.

"Get a towel and stop the blood," Adams said before fainting.

"He revived when Mrs. Adams took his head in her arms," Reed said in the trial.

"Then what did he say?" a defense attorney later asked.

"He was abeggin' me and her [Mrs. Adams] to help him live," Reed said.

According to a 1932 issue of the *Lubbock Avalanche-Journal*, two twelve-year-old girls, Brooksie Nell Echer and Georgia Mae Yeager, were walking home from school when the shooting occurred. "We were walking down the alley back of the doctor's office when we heard the first shot," Echer said.

In a crowded courtroom, in front of both the Adams and Tudor families, as well as members of the press and court officials, Echer bashfully testified to what she saw on the day the two peeked through the windowpanes of Dr. Adams's office.

"I looked and I saw smoke and the figure of a man," the young girl said. "I glanced in, but I don't know whether Georgia Mae did or not, and I saw a man standing there. I heard a voice and it said, 'Oh please don't shoot, please don't shoot me anymore.'"

"We heard the shot and started running," Georgia Mae said. "We heard someone say, 'Oh please don't shoot me.'"

The two ran toward the bank, and when they got to the corner of the bank, east of the doctor's office, Echer said, "We turned around and I saw Mr. Tudor give Mr. Abel a gun and he said, 'I shot Dr. Adams.'"

Julia Ann Price Adams held her husband's body as he died in her arms on a tragic and chaotic afternoon in 1932 on the Slaton Town Square. *Photo from the Slaton Town Square Antique Mall and Museum.*

Inside the office, F.J. Hilders, a farmer renting Dr. Adams's farm, was making his way into the office at the time of the ordeal. He said he heard the defendant say, "You killed my boy." He got to the door and heard Dr. Adams call out to him.

"The doctor was on his all-fours on the floor," Hilders said. Hilders then telephoned another doctor and helped Adams get to a seat.

Shortly after Reed made his way into the office, after witnessing Tudor hand over the gun to Sheriff Abel, Dr. Adams's wife, Julia Ann, arrived to help console her dying husband. Reed said Dr. Adams continued begging them to keep him alive.

"What were his exact words?" defense attorney J.E. Vickers asked.

"He said, 'Keep me to live long enough to kill the b-----,'" Reed said.

Reed claimed Mrs. Adams reprimanded the doctor for his remark.

"Don't die with that in your heart, Doctor," Mrs. Adams rebuked.

Dr. Adams rested in Julia Ann's arms as blood flowed from his body and onto her.

The same woman Dr. Adams had seen from across a crowded room during a church meeting in 1905 held him in the chaos; she peacefully assisted in calming her husband as he freed himself from the dry lands and baked countryside, finding solace in death.

A Father's Journey, 1932

On a late August afternoon in 1932, at the Englewood Cemetery in Slaton, Woodie Tudor was laid to rest.

Family and friends gathered in the small cemetery and remembered a young man, thirty years old, who adored his mom, his wife and his children but, most of all, his father, R.L. Tudor.

R.L. watched as his son was buried beneath a copper-colored stone. Surrounding the grave were the few wildflowers that had survived the Dust Bowl; they bloomed across fields and grew unruly like the untamed anger raging within R.L.'s psyche after the accidental death of his son.

On most days, over commonplace chatter and sundry pleasantries, Woodie Tudor had visited his father.

On August 25, 1932, Woodie, his wife and their children were driving to R.L.'s house before the entire family was to spend an afternoon at the Johnson Ranch, like they had done many times before.

"R.L. and his son were great old pals," J.W. Nesbitt, a close friend of both R.L. and Dr. Adams said during the trial. In a 1932 issue of the *Lubbock Avalanche-Journal*, he said he saw Woodie Tudor on the day of his death and declared that the boy appeared to be in good health.

Thirty minutes after Woodie was to be at R.L.'s house, R.L. learned that Woodie and his family had been involved in a car accident, and they were at Dr. Loveless's office.

R.L. arrived at the doctor's office to find Dr. Loveless "whittling on a stick," as was stated in the newspaper article. Woodie sat in a chair with a broken arm.

"Dad, I'm shore glad I didn't hurt the baby," Woodie said.

"Why have you been waiting here for so long?" R.L. asked his son.

"We're waiting on Dr. Adams," Woodie answered.

R.L. testified that he went to Dr. Adams's office and said, "My God, Dr. Adams, get over there and help my boy."

"You're talking to the wrong man," Dr. Adams said, according to R.L. "If you want that boy's arm treated, bring him over here. You all know I am the Santa Fe doctor and you ought to come here for treatment."

When Woodie was taken to Dr. Adams's office, R.L. said Woodie told the doctor he could not take ether. "Dr. Miller over at Clovis told me my heart would never stand it and never to take it," Woodie said.

"Yes, you can stand it," Dr. Adams told Woodie.

"Doctor, if that boy can't stand ether. Don't give it to him," R.L. said.

"I can stand it without the ether," Woodie said.

"We'll have to give it. Let's get going and get it over with," Dr. Adams said to Dr. Loveless, who assisted Adams in treating Woodie.

As they began to give the ether, Woodie said, "I love my daddy. I love my daddy."

"And that's the last words he [Woodie] said," R.L. testified in court. R.L. testified that Dr. Adams and Dr. Loveless gave Woodie two cans and part of a third of the anesthetic before he lost consciousness. "I went around to his face and said, 'My God son, come out of it, come out of it," R.L. recalled with an occasional tear falling down his cheek.

It was later, on October 13, that R.L. confronted Dr. Adams at his office.

"I wanted to try to get him to help take care of those babies [Woodie's two young children]," R.L. testified. "I felt he was responsible for his death through negligence."

R.L. said he walked into the office, spoke to the doctor and said he wanted to know, "What he was going to do with those babies?"

"I'm not going to do anything," Dr. Adams sternly said to R.L. "Get out and stay out."

"I just kept shooting," R.L. said. "After he told me to get out, I just kept shooting and he fell on his knees and I went out the door and gave myself up."

When the community arrived to bury Dr. Adams in mid-October 1932, almost the entire town showed up to pay their respects and mourn the pioneer doctor, who was buried beneath a granite tombstone with the name

"Adams" etched into the classic white stone that stood illuminated against the sun.

As the citizens of Slaton gathered to inter their hometown hero, across from the somber crowd, only a few steps away, sat the lonely grave of Woodie Tudor, bearing a tombstone etched in gothic calligraphy with the words "Gone, but not forgotten."

In a four-day trial, the jury found R.L. guilty of murder. The judge sentenced him to only two years in jail because of the circumstances surrounding the crime.

R.L. Tudor is buried next to his son in Englewood Cemetery.

Cecil Scott's Story, 2008

Born in 1908 in Vernon, Texas, Cecil Scott made his way to Slaton in 1919 by way of a Ford Model J pickup truck, only eight years after Slaton officially became a town.

On January 9, 2008, Scott woke to his 100th birthday. "I never really did accomplish anything, just took up space," Scott joked about his centennial birthday. "Lots of people turn 100 everyday."

"He doesn't think it's a big deal," Jeanna Smith, Scott's caregiver stated, "but this man has so many stories."

"Well, we got into Slaton at around ten or eleven in the morning in 1919. I was just a little boy," Scott said. "My daddy got us rooms at the Singleton Hotel. There we stayed about two or three weeks." Scott's father eventually got a job, and the family moved into their first home on South Thirteenth Street.

Scott started school in Slaton, where he walked ten blocks everyday to get to the building that housed grades one through twelve. School was held in a two-story building where Cathelene Thomas Elementary now stands.

"There were maybe about one hundred students in the school," Scott said, "and I liked all of the teachers. They were all very nice." The principal at the time was H.M. Pevehouse, and the superintendent was C.L. Stone. Scott eventually became a member of the Slaton Tiger Football Team.

"At one time the city dads were really interested in the athletic program, especially in football," he said. "They had a meeting and moved a family to Slaton to play for the Tigers. When the players got here they were twenty-five or thirty years old. Boy we went to town that year."

It was during his senior year with the class of 1930 that a young woman by the name of Pauline Margaret English came into his life. On June 11, 1932, she became his wife. He built a house on West Lynn in which the two would spend seventy-six years together, raising two daughters and making it their home.

Shortly after high school and during his marriage, Scott worked for the pharmacy. During those eight years, he also ran the movie theater on the side. "I used to exchange parts [from the theater] with the theater manager in Lubbock," Scott said. "He'd run over here all the time and I'd run over there." At the time, Slaton was home to two movie theaters. "We had a good town until they paved the road from here to Lubbock."

On December 7, 1941, Scott returned home from quail hunting. "I came in for some lunch and was told about [Pearl Harbor]." It was at that moment that Scott realized he would be going to fight in the war. "My first thought was that I would be in the army for a very long time."

Scott served in World War II, stationed in the Philippines and fighting on the front lines in New Guinea. "It's always a rough time when a war is going on," he said.

Scott worked for the post office for thirty-seven years upon his return.

"When we moved here [to Slaton], there was no water system, sewer systems or paved streets. I remember seeing a windmill in everyone's yard

In honor of the town's incorporation in 1911, a parade makes its way down Texas Avenue in 1936 in celebration. *Photo from the Slaton Town Square Antique Mall and Museum.*

and I thought that was just neat," Scott said. "There was this one year all the men grew their beards out for a year, just for something to do."

Scott devoted many hours to collecting stamps and coins and has taken many fishing trips to Del Rio, Texas. "We went to Canada a couple of times and on a cruise," Scott said. "We even went to Washington D.C., once. But I just grew up here and stayed. I guess I'm just used to being at home."

Remembering Grandpa, 2010

The 1860s. Texas. Three boys watched their parents become of no more value than a cellphone by today's standards. They were treated no better than a day-old newspaper or a stray dog. The sounds of chains rattling and the boisterous calls of men filled the thick woodlands air. They were the sounds of a customary East Texas slave trade.

According to an article in *The Slatonite* in 1970, A.D. Ridley remembered hiding in old "cat chimneys" when buffaloes came around. He stayed there for hours, until the buffaloes went away so he could go home. He lived in a log cabin with boarded-up windows because the Indians shot arrows through open windows.

Most of Ridley's stories, however, were locked away and heard only by a select few. Louise Johnson, his granddaughter, was one of those few.

"We'd just sit around, you know, and just talk," Johnson said from her home filled with typical twenty-first-century fare: Sponge Bob Square Pants plate settings for her grandchildren, a crystal globe plant-watering device placed in a fern and a cellphone next to her arm. A floral fragrant candle was lit and sat at the center of the table. "We'd climb up in the bed with him, and he'd tell us his stories."

Johnson spoke of being a young girl and going to her grandparents' humble two-room home. There, she and A.D.'s other granddaughters, Edith Fields and Pearlie Hill, listened to the stories of their grandfather, escaped slave A.D. Ridley.

Although an article from *The Slatonite* claimed that Ridley was one hundred years old in 1970, marking his birth on January 6, 1870, many of his relatives believed he was much older. There is no known birth certificate for him, and his parents' documentation was lost in the slave trade.

In the late 1800s, sometime before 1865, it is believed that a nine-month-old A.D. Ridley, along with his two older brothers, Louis and Arthur, watched as their parents were sold away to a Texas plantation. One night, Ridley's brothers decided to take a risk and ran away from the slave owner and their very own parents with the young A.D. in their arms. They never turned back.

"Uncle Louis was the oldest," Johnson said. "The three stuck together."

It is believed that the boys were living in Indian Territory in the 1870s. In 1874, the U.S. Army launched Red River War, which ended the Texas-Indian Wars. The Ridley boys found themselves dodging arrows.

In 1891, A.D. came across a young Native American woman by the name of Lula Lee Terry. The two were married in Red River County, where they lived on a plantation.

"They were servants in a big house," Pearlie Hill, another of Ridley's granddaughters, said. "The master fed them like animals. They would throw corn bread in the trough and pour buttermilk over it."

Many years after the Emancipation Proclamation and Texas was readmitted into the Union, black servitude continued to be a common practice on Texas plantations and farms.

"I remember my granddaddy saying he had a wagon and, with what little bit he had, they left the plantation," Hill said. "They were free to leave, and he left."

The couple made their way to Blossom, Texas, for an unknown number of years. "They would have to walk miles to school," Johnson said of the Ridleys and their children. "They would ride in a horse-drawn buggy to church."

In 1941, the Ridley family decided to move to Slaton.

Four years later, in 1945, Lula died.

"I remember my grandmother," Johnson said. "I was really young when she died, but I remember her long, black hair."

Johnson said her grandfather was a gentle soul who never raised his voice. She remembered going to help him pick cotton once, and the children found a tree filled with ripe peaches to snack on. "Now children," he told them gently. "Now those aren't your peaches to be picking."

The Davis Hotel, referred to as the "Negro Hotel" by *The Slatonite* in 1950s Slaton. *Photo from the Alton Kenney collection.*

"He never said a harsh word," Johnson said.

Although Ridley and his family lived in a segregated Slaton, Johnson said, "He would go uptown and trade at a few stores."

In the 1950s, even after escaping slavery, Indian warfare and the separation of his family, A.D. was only allowed to enter a select few places in Slaton.

"But he was never a complainer," Johnson said.

Johnson remembered some of the life lessons Ridley passed down to her. She remembered his gentle voice sometimes telling her, "Now you cherish the bridge you cross because you may just have to cross back over it."

"God has been so good to the black race," Johnson said, with the same insight of her grandfather. "We can make it off of a little bit of everything."

Slaton's History of Death, 1912

There's Slaton. There's Englewood Cemetery. And then there's Potters' Field. The history of death in Slaton began one year after the birth of the town, in 1912.

On a spring day, May 10, 1912, a small family gathered and buried their infant son, J.W. Obrian. In some documents, the name is spelled Ohrien, a spelling mistake that has confused many for nearly a century because, after all these years, the child who may or may not have been the firstborn of a family who left many years ago was the first person buried in Slaton.

Although the history and legend of this family remain mysterious, it is easy to imagine the anguish, grief and pain the family felt the day they buried an infant son on the lush, green plains, with striking purple and yellow wildflowers surrounding the small, lonely grave and soft spring breezes coaxing prairie grass to flutter.

According to *Slaton's Story*, A.E. Howerton operated the first funeral establishment. The first funeral home, which may have helped prepare the young body, began in Slaton earlier in 1912. It is believed to have been located in a small building one street over from Texas Avenue, where the VFW building's parking lot is now situated. It is not known where deceased pioneers were buried prior to the opening of the cemetery and the first funeral home. It is believed many were buried on private lands.

The second structure to house the local funeral home was opened in 1922 at 235 South Ninth Street. The building, which still stands, was constructed by Dr. and Mrs. E.C. Foster, who operated a furniture store alongside the funeral home. Many important and prominent citizens were respectfully remembered in this building, including members of some of the original families, such as the Brewers, Pembers and Dr. Sam Houston Adams.

On December 23, 1936, after second and third additions were made to the building, Mr. Webber Beauregard Williams moved his family into the upstairs living area of the building. Mr. Williams became the third owner of Slaton funeral homes.

"Moving from a residence in the new addition of Spur and into a funeral home on the highway through town was quite a transition," Glynna Englund, Williams's daughter, wrote in *Slaton's Story*. "We adjusted." Glynna Englund lived in the upstairs residence of the old funeral home until her recent death.

On May 2, 1944, the funeral home was left, in tragic irony, without a director. Mr. Williams died at the age of forty-seven after his second heart attack. At the time, and still today, Texas laws required that anyone operating a funeral home must be a licensed funeral director.

"Through efforts of area funeral director friends," Glynna wrote, "Mrs. Williams took her state board examination at an unscheduled time and, was licensed within a few months after Mr. Williams' death."

In 1944, it is stated in *Slaton's Story* that Glynna graduated from Slaton High School. She was studying journalism at Texas Tech University when she met her future husband, Bud Englund. After marriage, the two moved to Dallas, where Bud entered the Dallas Institute of Mortuary School. Glynna received her funeral director's license in 1948.

Glynna's sons, Dubbin and Robert, and grandson, Brett, currently operate the funeral home at its present location west of Englewood Cemetery.

The entrance to Englewood Cemetery is one of dignity and respect for the many who came before. Rows of large to meager tombstones, with names, decorative motifs and final inscriptions that offer clues about loved ones buried beneath Texas soil, spread across yards of sacred ground.

According to state records, the cemetery was established by the Santa Fe Railway. It is believed that the infant son of Slaton's first burial in the 1912 Englewood Cemetery was a member of a railroad family.

However, that is purely speculation, just like the origins of the name of the cemetery: Englewood.

To this day, there are a few theories but no accurate explanation for the naming of the cemetery.

"We lived south of Posey until 1918," W.J. Klattenhoff wrote in *Slaton's Story*. "We were there when the older Mr. Posey and his son died in a silo accident along with two Mexicans who tried to rescue them."

If Mr. Posey and his son were buried in Slaton, their bodies would be interred in the peaceful gardens of Englewood.

However, the two unknown Mexicans who gave their lives in trying to save the pair would have been laid to rest in Potters' Field, an emerging and stripped piece of land that lies beyond a tree-lined path and has estranged the departed for almost a century.

There were acting Jim Crow laws in Texas state parks beginning in the late 1800s. However, in 1923, Lubbock County passed an initiative to include the segregation of cemeteries. Slaton officials followed county initiatives.

Potters' Field is a once-detached piece of land that tells a separate story as mysterious as the name Englewood itself.

The land is filled with homemade tombstones of concrete, wood and, in some cases, chipped seashells. The majority of graves remain unmarked and, with just the faint sunken outlines of old graves, barren fields encompass the area where unknown human remains lie for eternity.

Potters' Field exists because the town needed to bury the unfortunate and poverty-stricken, as well as minorities. The cemetery was segregated for many years, and because of family lineage, it may seem the same way today.

There's Slaton. There's Englewood Cemetery. And then there's Potters' Field.

Ysaura Flores's Story, 2009

In 1915, then six-year-old Ysaura Flores didn't want to get left behind. In 1999, at the age of ninety, she faced a similar dilemma.

Flores was born in 1909 in a small Mexican village. The Mexican Revolution of 1910 and the civil war that followed left many Mexicans homeless and struggling. Flores remembered, as a child, hiding in a basement with relatives as the generals searched houses and villages.

"We were watching *The Alamo* once," Flores's daughter, Frances Cabrera, said. "She began wiping tears from her eyes and said, 'When I was a little girl, those men scared me.'" She spoke of the war and the generals who forced her family into hiding during her first six years on earth.

The revolution displaced many rural Mexican communities; some have estimated that nearly one in ten Mexicans immigrated to the United States because of the abundant wealth afforded to them in manufacturing jobs and the many agricultural opportunities during World War I.

"She remembers men in red garments coming to their home," Cabrera said in a 2009 interview. "She moved to the U.S. through Laredo with her grandmother in 1915."

Cabrera said, however, that due to a traumatic situation while crossing, she never had the desire to return.

According to Cabrera, for unknown reasons, Flores's family was permitted to cross, but authorities said she would have to be left behind. At the age of six, she had to discover a way to cross the border without the help of her family, who left her in Mexico.

That night, a young woman befriended Flores and helped her cross over the next day to join her family. She spent the rest of her life in Texas. "She never wanted to go back," Cabrera said.

Flores remained an illegal immigrant until marrying a musician named Manuel Flores at the age of twenty-six. It is unknown if she ever attended school, but she does know how to read Spanish and, after much practice, now English.

To support her family, she worked in the fields for many years picking cotton and onions and ridding the cotton fields of weeds. "There have been times when I have caught her lifting one-hundred-pound bags of cotton," Cabrera said. She also said that her mother often planted cotton in the front yard and still loves the feel of the bolls.

Flores was twenty-six when she bore her first child, and later, at the age of thirty, she gave birth to Cabrera. She also raised Manuel's other three children, whom he brought with him into their marriage. Today, the Flores family is made up of twenty-five grandchildren and many great-grandchildren.

Cabrera, who retired from the health field as a medical technologist, later joined the Peace Corps and was stationed in current-day Congo. "I was there for two and a half years," she said. Within the family, there are five nurses, one welder and her grandson, Joe Gonzales, who was named 2008 Slaton Man of the Year.

According to Cabrera, Flores is active in her church, Our Lady of Guadalupe. She makes sure to walk the three blocks every Sunday for Mass. "Some of the neighborhood kids ask her where she's going. 'To church,' she always says," Cabrera said.

In 1997, at the age of ninety, Flores was, once again, left behind.

Cabrera said that every year the priest took a group of elderly women to vote in local and national elections, and Flores hated to be left behind. Because she was not a citizen, Flores had not been allowed to vote for the majority of her life. "I asked her," Cabrera said one day when she realized how upset her mother was when she wasn't allowed to go. "Do you want to become a citizen?"

"Yes, I do," Flores said.

For two years, Cabrera and her mother spent countless hours studying American history and customs. "I was so scared for her," Cabrera said. "I didn't think she would do so well…She sat, waiting for her turn, she had her rosary in her hand. She was so calm, I couldn't believe it."

On October 13, 1999, Flores walked into the immigration office and found herself taking an oral exam to become a citizen. "She only missed one question," Cabrera said. "It was something we didn't study, but she was sworn in there on the spot."

Immediately following the exam, Flores asked Cabrera if she could now vote. "You have to register," Cabrera told her.

"Well, then lets go," Flores said.

In 2000, Flores voted in her first election. She has voted in every election since.

The Ladies of the Civic Culture Club, 1939

Within the red clay lands west of the Pecos River, a feisty young woman named Emma Lenorah lived in a half dugout with her husband, A.B. Robertson. This is where the story of one of Slaton's first pioneering women begins.

Typical rural housing in the late 1800s consisted of small wooden cabins or dugouts built into the rough terrain of the rugged West Texas hills and canyons. The people who lived on this land were often ranchers, who shared this piece of the Wild West with other species and cultures like scorpions, diamondback rattlesnakes and the last of the few remaining cowboys.

A Mexican cowboy, alone and injured on the range, knocked on the door of the Robertsons' dugout.

"[Emma Robertson] bathed and doctored his wound," *Slaton's Story* records. "She gave him food so he could continue on his way."

The young cowboy wore a necklace with a "crude carving of a human face." In gratitude for her hospitality, he handed the necklace over to Mrs. Robertson.

"This is my God," he said. "If you should ever be in any kind of trouble, all you have to do is show this God."

Accepting the gift, Mrs. Robertson placed it in her handbag.

Two months later, a short time before the young couple moved to Slaton, they made their way to San Angelo for business matters.

"Mr. Robertson had just sold some cattle and was carrying some sizeable amount of cash," the essay in *Slaton's Story* stated. "As they approached a creek which they had to cross they were halted by a Mexican who was armed with a rifle."

Not understanding what he was saying, Mr. and Mrs. Robertson stood frightened and confused. "While Mr. Robertson was trying to carry on a conversation with the man Mrs. Robertson reached into her handbag, took out the God and held it out to the Mexican," the article in *Slaton's Story* continued.

It is written that soon after seeing the necklace, the man bowed low, indicated with his hand for them to proceed, mounted his horse and rode away.

Years later, in 1910, Mr. Robertson acquired ranching properties in Lynn, Lubbock, Crosby and Garza Counties. In 1911, Mr. and Mrs. Robertson built a large, two-story brick home eight miles east of Slaton.

As Slaton slowly became an established town, it was Mrs. Robertson who, according to an article in *The Slatonite* in March 1939, helped erect many of the storefronts on Texas Avenue.

"No Alice-sit-by-the-fire, this tiny bundle of energy and high spirits, Mrs. A.B. Robertson's thoughts are of the future," the editor of *The Slatonite* wrote of the pioneer woman in 1939.

Of course, in 1939, Mrs. Robertson was not the only woman at the forefront of developing the small town into a productive city on the plains. *The Slatonite* also wrote of another organization that helped in the development of the community:

> *In the early days of Slaton's existence, while men were getting established in their professions and occupations, the women desiring to contribute their bit to the town's development, began promoting the social and civic life. The first step in this direction was the organization of the Civic and Culture Club.*

This women-only organization is credited with the establishment of home economics education in the Slaton public schools, planting shrubbery in the county park, leading the project to construct a city hall and conducting "pretty lawn contests" in order for Slaton to maintain its welcoming presence and beauty.

"Then came the World War," the article stated. "Their time was devoted entirely to Red Cross work."

The work of the Civic and Culture Club was such a vital part of the lifeline of the town that it became a dynamic foundation in the establishment of Slaton during the Depression and the following years.

The popularity of the group's work spread throughout the region, and on March 13, 1939, the City of Slaton received a letter from one of the most powerful women in the world:

> *I am very glad to send this note of congratulations and good wishes to the women of Slaton. I hope very much that they will be able to keep up the good work they have started.*
> *Very sincerely yours,*
> *Eleanor Roosevelt*

With this kind of encouragement, the Civic and Culture Club thrived. Lead by Julia Ann Adams, wife of the late Dr. Sam Houston Adams, the organization is also credited with organizing the annual Fourth of July Festival, establishing Triangular Park near the Santa Fe station, beautifying the Slaton school campuses and raising thousands of dollars to send various Slaton students to college.

"The club's interest turned to some of the outstanding needs of Slaton's Young People," *The Slatonite* reported.

> *Junior clubs were organized by committees from the Civic and Culture Club whereby more than one hundred girls have been directed in a worthwhile social and educational trend. A Student Loan Fund of $500 has been created, eleven Slaton boys and girls having already borrowed from this fund. Some of these young people are now teaching in Texas schools, others have entered the business world.*

Eventually, the city moved beyond the hard days of the Depression, and the skies were again bright blue. Slaton citizens had survived the ravage of the Dust Bowl's deadly grip. The people of Slaton found new forms of amusement, bringing in carnivals to entertain the thousands of people who worked in the surrounding fields. Visitors came to the town for its movie theaters, shopping centers, bakery and festivals; the future of Slaton was bright.

Of course, in March 1939, when television had not yet been introduced as a vital household product, the only means of electronic news was via the radio. Yet only a few could afford the gadget. *The Slatonite* was the town's main source for national and world events.

Abe Kessel, seen here in the 1930s, made his home in Slaton after escaping Czarist Russia in the early 1900s. He opened a chain of variety stores across West Texas and throughout the South Plains. *Photo from* Slaton's Story.

A small article in *The Slatonite* stated in a press release from Washington, "We, as a people, are angry about what Hitler has done. But again; we can do nothing more than protest, because the United States has no business going to war over some other nation's troubles."

The War Years, 1941–1945

In 1941, it was official: the Depression was over. Celebrations, which were once halted during the Dust Bowl doldrums and the menacing Depression era, continued once again beneath the blue West Texas skies.

Music drifted across the humble town square, bounced off brick buildings and wafting between trees. The spring air was overcome with laughter, pleasantries and the anticipative hints of young love.

"I married a Slaton boy and moved to Slaton," Mary Helen Meeks said in a recent interview from the Slaton Care Center.

Mary Helen, who worked as a telephone operator in 1941, on many occasions took in the sights and sounds of Slaton. Her hometown, however, was the neighboring town of Post.

It was on one of those typical concert-filled afternoons that Mary Helen, sitting with a friend on the lawn of the town square, looked across the grassy field and locked eyes with a stranger who changed her forever.

After approaching the man and exchanging light conversation, Mary Helen rushed home and told her sister, "I met the man I am going to marry."

Of course, remembering only his eye color and his name after that first meeting, Mary Helen returned to the square and to the concerts many more times, and a few months after that first meeting with Alton, she became Mrs. Alton Meeks.

According to *Slaton's Story*, Alton was the son of Roy and Sue Meeks, who lived on a farm in the north end of Slaton. Roy was a farmer and a cattle

A traveling carnival makes a stop in 1940s Slaton. *Photo from the Alton Kenney collection.*

The Slaton High School band, seen here in 1937, often entertained citizens by performing concerts on the town square. *Photo from the* Tigers Lair, *1937.*

buyer for many years. It is written that during the Depression, "Mrs. Meeks and the boys peddled milk, butter, eggs and frying chickens all over Slaton."

When Mary Helen and Alton married, the two left their farm life in exchange for the small-town atmosphere. Living at 250 West Dickens, Mary Helen worked as a bookkeeper at the Slaton Co-op Gin.

"Slaton wasn't much different in 1941 than it is today," Mary Helen said. "Just a small country town. Some places have gone out of business and some have come in."

A few months later, in the fall of 1941, many citizens gathered and cheered on the Slaton football team at Tiger Stadium. The crowd would also sometimes travel by train to watch the Tigers play against other rival teams, such as Lamesa and the 1939 Texas state champions, Lubbock High.

The movie theaters on the town square also flourished, as patrons from other towns and farmworkers made their way every weekend to shop, dine and catch a show.

Entertainment became a vital part of the local economy. On some afternoons, the town's skyline rose with the carnival rides of visiting jamborees that came by train, daring young people to take a whirl and experience new thrills on merry-go-rounds and Ferris wheels.

In 1941, a young woman named Mary Enloe arrived in Slaton. She lived on a farm with her family, who raised livestock and harvested vegetables.

In the 1930s, many traveled to the Slaton Town Square to shop, eat and socialize. *Photo from* The Slatonite *archive.*

"We also planted cotton," Enloe said in a 2010 interview from the Slaton Care Center. "Then there were the watermelons," she added. "They were pretty good."

Enloe remembered many of the festivals held in Slaton during the 1940s:

> *I remember one time when I borrowed my grandmother's old dress, buttoned up shoes and a bonnet. They called that festival Pioneer Days. The festival was held downtown and they made food and ice cream. I remember the ice cream.*

By 1941, the radio was a household item, and families gathered around it listening to music, news and variety show programming. This was also the year a talented five-year-old boy by the name of Charles Hardin Holley (he later changed his name to Buddy Holly) won a talent show in the neighboring city of Lubbock by singing the song, "Have You Ever Gone Sailing (Down the River of Memories)."

As people listened on the radio to the music that entered their homes, a blunt voice broke through the airwaves, and the music was sharply halted. It was December 7, 1941. A man's voice blared from radios throughout Slaton: "We interrupt this program to announce that the Japanese have attacked Pearl Harbor, Hawaii."

"I remember [Pearl Harbor] very well," Mary Helen said. "We had the radio on all day and just sat around listening to the news."

Christine Jackson, another resident of the Slaton Care Center, also remembered the frightening day. "It was terrifying," she said in a 2010 interview. "We thought the war was going to come to us."

Although war never came to Slaton, in many aspects, like most other American cities and towns, Slaton went to war.

In the spring of 1942, one year after marrying Mary Helen, Alton Meeks scurried through the house, searching high and low in the family's backyard, even scourging the trash cans, for scrap pieces of metal.

"My husband tried to gather metal from everywhere," Mary Helen said.

He wasn't the only one; the entire community of Slaton came together to challenge the entire country in becoming the city that could collect the most scrap metal.

"We have the most patriotic citizens in the United States right here in Slaton," D.R. Reid, chairman of the Slaton Salvage Committee, said in the July 31, 1942 edition of *The Slatonite*.

> *We will challenge New York, Chicago and Lubbock combined. Of course, it will have to be on per capita basis but just let us at 'em and we will show the world that we are the best Salvage collectors that ever rounded up old water bottles or broken down cans.*

By 1942, it was official: the world was at war.

The Scrap Is On

In the summer of 1942, Slaton was war ready.

"The scrap is on," Odie Hood, a member of the Slaton Scrap Drive committee, said in an issue of *The Slatonite* in 1942. "I, for one, am full of hot blood and ready to fight."

He wasn't alone in his sentiments.

Royce Pember said in that same article, "It is hardly right to wake the folks in Lubbock up from a long sleep, but it is going to be a battle to the finish and I say we've got the advantage if we all do our part."

W.H. Rogers, a member of the Texas Salvage Committee, said that each town could use any method considered the best by committee members to collect the old metals and rubber.

"The local committee is making arrangements to tag every man, woman and child who donates any item of metal or rubber," an article in *The Slatonite* read. "Those who do not bring metal or rubber will be asked to buy a defense stamp; those who refuse to do either, will be forced to hang their heads in shame."

The Slaton Chamber of Commerce also did its part in aiding the war effort.

On July 28, 1942, at the chamber meeting, a series of projects was introduced that would stimulate the city's progress, as well as aid in wartime efforts.

"A motion was introduced and passed to keep a supply of post cards at the canteen at the Santa Fe Station," an article in *The Slatonite* read. "The post cards are to be given to the troops passing through Slaton."

Another addition to the bustling railroad town that brought in thousands of troops during the height of the war years was the approval of the USO reading room at the depot.

"Briggs Robertson reports that he has been notified by the USO that an authorization of $100 per month has been allowed for the operation of a lounge at the Santa Fe Depot," *The Slatonite* stated. The room was to be furnished "for men who are routed through Slaton."

Fitted by local contributions, and operated by the women of Slaton, men and women from various parts of the country on their way to aid in the war effort found comfort and various forms of entertainment while waiting in Slaton. "The reading room will offer a limited amount of entertainment for the service men, such as magazines and radio programs." The town also developed extensive advertisement efforts for the troops to remember that they were welcome to return to Slaton at the end of their tours.

As various troops passed through Slaton, marching toward the town square for the various entertainment offerings and free treats at the Slaton Bakery, many passed the variety of shops, confectionaries, clothing stores and movie theaters that moved the bustling little city into the 1940s—a time many Slatonites consider the city's heyday.

In the 1940s, Slaton officials developed an elaborate advertisement campaign to attract soldiers who passed through Slaton by train on their way to fight in World War II. *Photo from* The Slatonite *archive.*

However, not all who arrived in Slaton were as optimistic as the troops who came to town.

On Halloween 1943, an eleven-year-old girl by the name of Dana Ross Smallwood sat in the bed of a pickup truck, riding backward for many hours across the bumpy Texas terrain, enveloped by the kicked-up dust, until they reached their destination: Slaton.

"Some of us rode backwards in the truck all the way from Canton, Texas, located in Van Zandt County," Dana wrote in *Slaton's Story*. "I was sick when we arrived so my first impression of this town wasn't very good."

After years of struggle in East Texas, Dana's father, Fagan, decided to move the family to a more prosperous region of the state. "My father went to work for Ray C. Ayers and Son," Smallwood wrote. The business later became known as Supreme Feed Mills.

Fagan worked diligently during the year of 1943, and by 1945, the family had bought their first home at 435 South Sixth Street. "After living in the country for eleven years," Smallwood wrote, "Slaton was quite a difference for us. Going to the show was a favorite pastime. It only cost 9 cents to enter the show and a bag of popcorn was only 5 cents."

Of course, the movie theater wasn't the only form of entertainment, and Smallwood wrote that some of her favorite days were when variety shows would come to town. "We always looked forward to when the Harley Sadler Tent Show would come to Slaton," she wrote. "The tent show was usually located in a vacant lot."

In the summer of 1943, however, as the students of the Slaton schools were on summer break, tragedy struck the vibrant town when the principal of East Ward School, which today houses the Stephen F. Austin Elementary, Mr. K.S. McKinnon, unexpectedly died. Earl Brasfield was elected to fill the position—a very challenging job.

"Because of World War II," *Slaton's Story* records, "the Kavanaugh administration was a trying one." The Kavanaugh administration refers to the superintendent of the schools during a time when Slaton had five different principals, including the late K.S. McKinnon. The other principals left for various career advancements.

"From 1942–45, the teacher shortage was very critical," *Slaton's Story* reported of the trying war years for the school system. "This situation was met by the hiring of local people who had been former teachers, and by permitting teachers living in Lubbock to commute."

Slaton's Story also reported that various school activities were postponed and suspended during the 1940s:

> *Football and band were discontinued in 1942. Football was reinstated in 1945 and band began again in 1947–48. Emphasis was placed on more patriotic activities, such as scrap metal drives, than on the regular routine of school life.*

One such activity many students participated in was the battle between Slaton and Lubbock to collect the most salvage possible in 1942. "Arrangements are being made to build storage near City Hall where all salvage will be donated to a war time charity organization," an article in a 1942 issue of *The Slatonite* read.

"This is just the beginning of a far reaching salvage campaign," *The Slatonite* article stated.

> *People all over the nation will be asked again to bring in everything possible to make guns, ships and planes for the armed forces. The challenge being issued by the Slaton Committee is the opening gun to start this section of the country on a Salvage Collecting program that will amaze the world.*

The Slaton Bakery, 1943

In 1943, the halting, crashing noise of train wheels screeching across steel tracks and the explosive sounds of steam trumpets warning of the train's arrival meant one thing: donuts.

Throughout the 1940s, trains routinely stopped in Slaton, and following the sweet and irresistible scent of freshly baked donuts and brownies that welcomed their arrival, young troops marched down Texas Avenue and made their way to the most famous landmark in town: the Slaton Bakery.

A young man named Johnny McCormick helped welcome the hundreds of troops who passed through town leaving to fight in the war. He was an employee at the Slaton Bakery from 1943 to 1945.

In the book *Slaton Bakery: Baking with Memories*, McCormick wrote that his job during the early half of the 1940s was to wrap bread, "which took about three to four hours each night."

However, his job was complicated when his friends visited.

"When my buddies would drop by," McCormick wrote, "they would grab a handful of brownies on their way out."

The owner of the bakery in 1943, Barney Wilson, was not pleased with their behavior. "Next time, you pay for their brownies," he told the young McCormick.

"Needless to say, this stopped my buddies from visiting," McCormick wrote.

By 1943, World War II was raging in Europe, and America was two years into the conflict after the surprise attack on Pearl Harbor in 1941.

The Slaton Bakery on the square offered free donuts to soldiers passing through town during World War II. *Photo from* Slaton's Story.

"During that era, there were several instances that affected the bakery," Max Wilson wrote in the same book. "Commodity rationing was in effect including sugar, fruit, gasoline, and tires to name a few."

It is written that Barney knew he would have plenty of gasoline ration stamps to be able to continue to deliver his bread around town. "He never had a problem with that," Max wrote, "but occasionally the sugar would run out before the month was out."

During this era, fruit was also in short supply because the government wanted to allocate all the canned fruit possible for the troops overseas.

"On a few occasions," Max wrote, "desperation prevailed." Barney often told his family of times when his only options for keeping Slaton's sweet tooth satisfied was to travel to Houston and buy fruit on the black market. "Cherries were hard to get and sometimes he had to substitute black plums for a mix with cherries for the pies and turnovers," Max wrote. "He told of making pineapple pies out of yellow squash."

However, the difficult times did not diminish the reputation of the Slaton Bakery. For many, it's hard to imagine Slaton without the sweet smell of donuts baking during the summer mornings, sugar cookies with bright pink frosting resting in cases on spring afternoons and thumbprint cookies, fresh from the oven, cooling on winter nights.

"It started when I was a small child," Brad Lamb wrote. "As far back as I can remember Daddy used to bring donuts and cookies home from The Slaton Bakery."

"Home and The Slaton Bakery are the same to my family and I," Rebecca Diane Howell wrote. "My first memory is pressing my nose up to the display case and taking in all those cookies, pies and pastries. Not to mention the familiar smells those goodies tempted you with."

According to *Slaton's Story*, the history of the bakery in Slaton dates back to June 1923, when two bakeries in the town consolidated. The bakery came under the ownership of a man named Mr. Brooks. However, Mr. Brooks's dreams of a bakery in Slaton were short-lived when the building he operated from burned down in 1927.

A new bakery reopened shortly after and was operated by the Star brothers, who sold it to a Mr. Carr in 1928, before it was sold to R.D. Hickman in 1929.

It was during Hickman's ownership that the popularity of the bakery rose as people made their way through Slaton by train.

"I worked at the bakery around 1939 and 1941," Calvin Lamb wrote. "Mr. Hickman owned the bakery and Barney was the baker."

Lamb wrote of a time when people would stand outside the bakery before noon, waiting for warm donuts to come out of the oven so they could have fresh donuts with their lunches.

"We also had fried pies that were ready about noon," Lamb wrote, "and people were eager to get them while they were hot."

Hickman would own the bakery for many years, until he was bought out by Barney in February 1943. Barney was the owner of the bakery during the Second World War.

"When Barney bought the bakery from Mr. Hickman," Ollie Mae Wilson, Barney's wife, wrote, "he worked very long hours. He didn't have time to come home for lunch. I would pack him a lunch in a brown paper bag."

"My mother was a silent partner with my father in business at The Slaton Bakery," Jimella Wilson Simpson wrote. "She was also a[n] unsung hero. I never heard her complain about the hard work. She kept house, cooked for the family and worked side by side with her husband to keep the business running smoothly. The Slaton Bakery was a true family endeavor with mother as the hub."

From behind the display cases filled with various types of cookies, pastries and sugary sweets of all sorts, alongside Barney and his employees, Ollie Mae also welcomed troops into Slaton during the war years and wished them well on their way.

"The troops would march down Texas Avenue on the square," Max wrote. "If we caught wind of it soon enough, Barney would set up free coffee, donuts, and sometimes brownies to give to the soldiers."

Other businesses on Texas Avenue, such as Shorty Mell's Café or Maxey's Café, furnished coffee for the young men asked to defend the world from the Nazi regime.

"Several soldiers that have passed through Slaton, retracing their journey during the war," Max wrote, "remembered this stop."

The Wilson family said that several veterans of World War II have revisited Slaton throughout the years. "We have had them come in and ask if this bakery was still the same family that had given them just a little something special during the war," Max wrote, "knowing that they may not be coming home."

Across the Great Plains, 1943

More than seven hundred miles separate Slaton, Texas, and Nebraska. The land stretching between the two states and across the Great Plains is similar, especially come autumn, when knee-high green plants bloom across the wide flatlands and blossom with white gold: cotton.

Ben Diaz and his family, including a young daughter named Sara Diaz, who was thirteen at the time, in search of fieldwork, migrated across the Great Plains throughout the 1930s. Sara, who often dressed in blouses made of feed sacks and pants of heavy material, worked in the fields with her siblings, with their father standing guard should there be rattlers.

"We pulled cotton," Sara said recently from her home filled with statues of saints and pictures of family members adorning the walls. A television set on a Spanish station was tuned to a telenovela in the background. "It's a lot different from picking cotton. We would reach down with both arms," she said, bringing her arms up midway as if preparing for a hug, "and pulled the cotton with both our arms and filled the sack. Picking cotton is when you pick the bulbs and clean the seeds out of them."

Slaton's Story records that Ben, Sara's father and a native of Mexico, married Delfina Hernandez in Taylor, Texas, on September 10, 1927. The couple bore seven children: Jesus, Ignacio, Sara, Joe, Moses, Librado and Juanita. The family migrated during harvest season but lived in Thorndale during their time off, while the children attended school for three months out of the year.

In 1947, as the family made their journey from Nebraska to Thorndale in South Texas, they passed through Slaton. Ben said to his wife, "I want you to look the town over with me."

In Slaton, Ben showed Delfina the town surrounded by cotton. He showed her the town square, the small shops and the movie theaters that had welcomed thousands before.

Two years after World War II ended, the town had returned to its small and humble atmosphere. The troops who once passed through by train were now long gone and were only memories in postwar Slaton.

"I would like to stay here," Ben said to his wife as the two discovered the town.

In November 1947, the Diaz family became Slaton's newest residents.

During their time in Slaton, the family worked at the Caldwell Farm. The children continued working the fields alongside their father. Sara said it was hard work, but it had to be done. "We did what Daddy said," she said. As a thirteen-year-old girl reared on farm work, she knew no other life.

Of course, the family found ways to entertain themselves in the fields, and during watermelon season, Sara said they often picked watermelons and ate them for lunch. "They were so sweet, I can still remember the taste," she said.

When the children did have time off, they made their way to the theaters on the town square. "Because of the color of our skin, the only other places, besides the movie theaters, we could walk into was the grocery store or drugstore," Sara said. Of course, even in the Slaton Theater, the only place Sara said they were allowed to sit was in the balcony. "We weren't allowed to use the concession stand," she said. "We would have to go to the restaurants and buy hamburgers to take with us," even though at the restaurants on the square, they were only allowed to use back entrances.

During the 1940s and well into the 1950s and '60s, Slaton, like the rest of the southern United States, was dominated by Jim Crow laws, which authorized the separation of the use of public facilities between white Americans and black Americans, lumping dark-skinned Mexicans in with the black Americans. Many restaurants in Slaton separated their patrons by race, and even city hall had separate water fountains reserved for white citizens and black citizens.

In the late 1940s, Ben Diaz tried stopping his vehicle before slamming into a soda machine that sat outside a filling station in Slaton. However, his attempt to stop proved futile, and he found his vehicle bumping the soda machine before coming to a complete halt.

The owner of the filling station was not pleased with the accident and rushed out to chastise Ben.

"You're going to have to pay for that," the man said to Ben as he looked at the damage with displeasure. "I want twenty dollars for it."

Ben, accepting the terms, told the man he would have to go to his house, which was miles away on a farm, and retrieve the cash. The man told him he would have to leave his car at the filling station until his return.

As Ben walked across town and onto the highway leading to his house, a friend of his, Luke Slone, stopped and asked why he was walking. When Ben told him of the altercation, Luke pulled a twenty-dollar bill out of his pocket, handed it to Ben and drove him to the filling station to retrieve his vehicle.

It is written in *Slaton's Story*, however, that though the family had their struggles in the new town, they did come to know and like some of the people. "We have acquired many friends through the years and it would be impossible to mention all of them," members of the family wrote in the book. "Dad will never forget the first man in Slaton to befriend him when he first came to Slaton. That man is Luke Slone."

Camaraderie between the community and the Diaz family slowly grew during their early years there.

Ben bought their first home from K.L. Scudder. Within a few years of knowing the family, Scudder approached Ben with an opportunity to reach out to the Spanish-speaking population of Slaton, which had grown during the height of the Bracero Program that began during World War II. The program brought many Mexicans to Slaton to work in the cotton fields, on the railroads and in various other agricultural ventures during the times of a weak workforce. The Presbyterian Church wanted to attract the Spanish speakers and thought Ben was the right man to reach out to the community.

"Dad was interested and he started to help by speaking to the people," the Diaz family wrote in *Slaton's Story*. United in faith, the people of the Presbyterian Church accepted Ben, and he later became a lay preacher.

Of course, the Diazes' beginnings at the church weren't as smooth and orderly as imagined.

When Sara walked into the church one afternoon, she noticed one of the congregants giving her a disdainful look, and then the woman, turning to

The Slaton Farm Store, seen here in the 1950s, was a thriving business on the Slaton Town Square. *Photo from* The Slatonite *archive.*

another member of the church, said within earshot of Sara, "I don't like people like that coming in here."

Sara turned toward the woman and said, "Rebecca, you're supposed to be a Christian and you feel this way about the color of my skin?" The woman looked down at Sara, shocked by her vigor. "If you go to heaven," Sara continued, "there'll be people who are my color."

Sara began walking away but then stopped in her tracks, turned toward the woman and said, "And if you go to hell, there'll be some of us there, too." She turned her back and continued walking.

Lights Out for the Forrest Hotel, 1953

For a brief moment, a light flickered in a second-story room of the two-story Forrest Hotel on the Slaton Town Square on a spring night in 1953. The light flickered, growing dim and bright again, before finally shutting out completely as H.H. Boyle's room, soon after the darkness, filled with white smoke.

That night, smoke also filled the rest of the building that sat on the corner of Ninth and Lubbock Streets. The twenty-five patrons occupying the building rushed out as the crackling fire spread.

Boyle, trying to make his way down a hallway to the stairs to find an escape, found the smoke too thick and the darkness all-consuming. He was trapped in the Forrest Hotel as fire quickly engulfed the building.

That following Friday, April 24, 1953, *The Slatonite* reported that the other patrons, fortunately, had made their way out of the burning building. "Miraculously enough," the article stated, "none of the hotel's approximately 25 guests suffered serious injury in the blaze, one of the worst ever recorded in the annals of Slaton history."

On that spring night, Wednesday, April 22, 1953, people were awakened shortly after midnight. They looked out windows and from their front yards at the smoke and blaze that drifted from their charming town square.

Even from the Slaton Club House, which was a few blocks down the red brick street, flames could be seen.

It was in that same building, the Slaton Club House, that only a few months earlier, in January 1953, the Reverend P.J. Burns had presented a plaque to L.B. Hagerman, Slaton's Man of the Year.

The Slatonite reported that more than 152 people attended the annual Chamber of Commerce Banquet. Hagerman was chosen as Man of the Year for his forty-two years as a "railroad man" in Slaton and his extensive work for the Boy Scouts of America. The event was emceed by Robert Hall Davis and ended in laughter and merriment. Davis ended by telling the crowd, "We hope all of you will remember Slaton as the fastest-growing city between Posey and Southland."

However, months later, the laughter was hushed as the Slaton Chamber of Commerce dealt with a town square in rubbles.

As the people staying at the Forrest Hotel rushed out, most losing their belongings in the fire, violent flames grew more and more unruly throughout the night and well into the morning.

Boyle had to make a decision. He had two options: face the uncertainty of running through hallways toward unpredictable flames and smoke-filled darkness or find his way out by other means.

The Slaton Town Square on Ninth Street, facing the Singleton Hotel, which later became the Forrest Hotel, circa 1920. *Photo from the Slaton Town Square Antique Mall and Museum.*

Boyle went to the window in his room, looked down at the alleyway below and jumped.

The fire began in the storeroom at the rear of Itty Bitty Drug. The fire was estimated to have caused $125,000 in damage, "perhaps more," according to *The Slatonite.*

"The lean, nervous and likeable Clyde Doherty, who owned the Itty Bitty for scarcely more than two years, stood heartbrokenly in front of his place of business as late as 4:20 am on Wednesday morning, sobbing ashamedly," *The Slatonite* reported.

As Boyle escaped the flames with a non–life threatening ankle injury, in the front of the hotel, people watched in awe, and a few voiced their grievance in the still of the warm spring night.

"It's everything I have ever worked for my whole life, it's gone," Doherty shouted as he watched the flames reaching farther and farther into the sky.

Many sat on the town square and watched as the fire soared into the night, and by the time the sun rose the next morning, all that remained of the top floor of the skeletal structure was the smoldering soot and ash of what once was many Slatonites' first memory of their fair city.

On that night, in Slaton, there was no laughter.

On Friday, when *The Slatonite* went to print, on the front page, the blaring headline that week read, "Midnight Holocaust Guts Forrest Hotel."

A Shooting in Pleasant Valley, 1961

Like a pesky mosquito, the stage lights buzzed annoyingly before the crowd of more than four hundred people in the Slaton High School Auditorium on the night of March 30, 1961. On the stage, an authoritative man stood and addressed the attentive crowd.

"Man's creative and productive genius can only thrive in a climate of freedom," C.L. Kay, a representative of Lubbock Christian College, said. Because it was not his first time addressing a large crowd, he spoke with an air of confidence.

The five-week seminar was sponsored by the Slaton Lion's Club and consisted of topics dealing with the looming threat and unsettling fear of communism and its connection to socialism.

A 1961 article in *The Slatonite* reported that Kay's seminar was educational and well known, as he had made many other appearances in other communities and would introduce a wealth of knowledge to the Slaton public.

"Mr. Kay reveals facts and information of many of the primary problems of today's society," *The Slatonite* reported, "including the continual perpetration of communism into the American way of life."

However, fifteen miles away from the festivities, a rural farming community remained abnormally silent after the previous week's bullet-infused events.

On Monday afternoon, March 20, 1961, J.O. Roberts knocked on the door of his farmhand Chester Tatum's dwelling, and a series of events unfolded that left Tatum lifeless on the concrete floor of his grimy accommodations.

All was well in Pleasant Valley, the farming community south of Slaton. The area, made up of sparse farms and mile after mile of cotton fields, was not an official town and had no law enforcement or post office. The people who knew of Pleasant Valley were those who lived in Pleasant Valley.

Many Slaton citizens had not heard of the unofficial town. However, on March 27, 1961, many in the community were shocked to see a photo of a dead body, covered by a white sheet, on the front page of their hometown newspaper.

The events began early that Monday when Tatum made a quick trip to the nearby city of Post and ended up in a hospital room.

"I can't imagine what's come over Will," Tatum said when police picked him up from roaming the streets of Post. Police officials in Post took Tatum to the local hospital.

Tatum, believed to be of sound mind, was released from the hospital and was taken back to his dwellings in Pleasant Valley.

"I can't imagine what's come over Will," Tatum continued repeating in the cop car as he was taken to the farm.

Tatum lived a solitary life and was known as a quiet and gentle man. He had worked on the farm for many years, and the few people who lived in Pleasant Valley were familiar with Tatum and his tranquil persona. "Tatum's wife had died 25 years ago," *The Slatonite* reported. "He lived alone behind the Roberts' home."

"He had always been a good employee," *The Slatonite* reported. "He was respected and well thought of by the Roberts family."

When not working, Tatum spent most of his days and nights alone in the three-room structure Mr. Roberts built for him out of concrete cinder blocks. During the winter months, Tatum kept warm beneath a bundle of used blankets the Roberts family provided. In the hot summers and warm springs, a window above his homemade twin bed cooled the space.

On that disastrous Monday afternoon in March, J.O. Roberts, aware of Tatum's stressful afternoon in Post, took a plate of food to his living quarters as he had done many times before.

"Go away," Tatum said when Roberts knocked on the door.

Confused by Tatum's insubordination, Roberts opened the door and was met with the bullet of a .38-caliber handgun to his abdomen. He fell to the floor and, for a brief moment, the afternoon remained serene, until Roberts's wife ran out of their farm home to find her husband on the ground outside Tatum's concrete home, holding his stomach as blood quickly spread through the front of his buttoned-up shirt.

The Slatonite reported that his wife, accompanied by a neighbor, took the farmer to the West Texas Hospital in Lubbock, where he was immediately admitted and remained in critical condition for a substantial amount of time.

Tatum sat alone and barricaded in his cinder-block quarters.

When cops arrived at Tatum's living quarters, Slaton police chief Eugene Martin tried talking to him through the open window. Tatum was uncooperative and responded with a shotgun blast from the window.

The bullet missed Martin, but gunpowder exploded across his face.

One of the officers who had accompanied Martin in his pursuit threw a tear gas bomb into the habitat, and gunshots continued from both sides. Another tear gas bomb was thrown into the structure. The explosive gunshots ceased.

When the cops entered, Tatum's lonesome body lay lifeless on the floor from a gunshot wound.

The next week, as the citizens of Slaton solemnly remembered the horrendous incidents that took place out in the fields they all now knew as Pleasant Valley, the rumors dissipated, and the chatter was once again pleasing. They listened to Kay's speech and his message of the communist and socialist threats that he believed plagued the world.

"America's greatness," Kay said before the conscientious crowd, "is the result of a moral society, constitutional government and the free enterprise system known as capitalism."

The program, entitled "The Freedom Seminar," hypnotized the Slaton crowd as Kay continued warning the people of the all-too-real and all-too-powerful communist threats to the livelihood of the pleasant lives to which Slatonites were accustomed.

"There is a need to remain alert," Kay gravely said.

The people indisputably listened, even though McCarthyism was already almost a decade past.

The Slaton Situation, 1961

Young women in gorgeous gowns elegantly walked across the stage in Slaton, wrapped in fluffy tulle. In 1961, Slaton was a bustling town where grocery, appliance and western stores took the place of the wild prairie flowers as the city prepared to celebrate fifty years of its existence.

Many citizens gathered on May 29 at the Slaton High School Auditorium and watched as young women were judged on their elegance, poise, sophistication and talent. Miss Slaton was to be chosen on that night of beauty.

"The young woman representing Miss Slaton during the Golden Anniversary Celebrations," an emcee said to the large crowd, "Miss Carolyn Rhoades."

Miss Slaton made many public appearances as the city's population doubled to more than twelve thousand visitors during the Golden Anniversary that summer. However, the men weren't left out of the festivities.

In honor of the old frontier pioneers, a beard-growing competition was held. Men all across town grew full beards, half beards or as much of a beard as they could, which for some, aside from a few stubbles, wasn't much. For that summer, men put away their razors and let the wild fur grow. The beards were judged during the festivities that took place on the town square.

Alongside the beard-judging festivities were various cookouts and barbecues sponsored by many of the town's organizations, and a parade traveled down the red brick roads of the Slaton Town Square.

"Slaton's festive and long-planned Golden Anniversary celebration will kick off June 8th," *The Slatonite* reported in 1961.

Kicking off the activities was a women's luncheon, where the women took to the town square dressed as pioneers. A two-day rodeo was held at Tiger Stadium, followed by a dance at the VFW Hall. A granite monument in the shape of Texas was given to the city and placed on the lawn of the town square.

After Ben Davis, a postal employee at the time, picked up his trophy for best beard in Slaton and the last of the confetti and thrown candy was swept from the streets, the people of Slaton went their separate ways.

However, for the local bowling league, it was back to work.

Five young Slaton men who called their team "The Smoothies" were the talk of the town in August 1961. Wearing rayon collared shirts and pressed slacks, with neatly combed hair, the team practiced for many hours at local bowling alleys.

In a national bowling tournament, The Smoothies of Slaton placed fourth among twelve thousand teams, and each took home a $700 check.

For The Smoothies, and the rest of the citizens in Slaton, that August was filled with the typical fare of a small town summer. Backyard cookouts were held with friends and family. Trips to Buffalo Lake were customary. Lounging beneath shaded trees in the county park was routine. For the youngsters of the town, the place to be in the summer of '61 was the city pool.

In late August, trying to absorb the final days of summer, a young Slatonite made his way to the city pool to enjoy an afternoon of swimming. Unbeknownst to many in the community, that person was denied entrance.

It wasn't until the summer months had passed and well into the winter of that year that the story first appeared in *The Slatonite*.

"A Slaton resident of Mexican descent—an American citizen, not a Mexican citizen, was refused entrance to the swimming pool, operated by the Board of City Development of tax funds, last August," *The Slatonite* reported in December 1961.

The article reported that a stern letter from government officials was sent to the mayor.

"Slaton was thrust into the spotlight of state notice this week when it was made public that the City Commission was ordered by the U.S. Department of Labor to integrate its municipal swimming pool or be refused the use of Mexican national labor," *The Slatonite* read.

Regional director of the Department of Labor Tracy O. Murrell wrote in a letter to city officials:

> *This is to advise that unless the city of Slaton takes corrective action to remove the discriminatory restrictions in connection with the use and operation of the municipal swimming pool within 30 days from the receipt of this certified letter, action will be instituted to remove any Mexican Nationals in the area and prohibit Mexican Nationals being contracted into the area.*

"We resent the government trying to ram something down our throats," the mayor said to *The Slatonite*.

Other farmers were not fond of the governmental actions used to fight discrimination in Slaton.

"We told the Department of Labor we would work something out, and I think we would have," a local farmer said. "They're just trying to put the squeeze on the Bracero Program and get it closed down entirely."

In response to the outrage, city officials wrote to the Department of Labor. Murrell sent another letter to the city of Slaton that stated, "Mexican Nationals cannot be recruited by the secretary to be employed in any area where there is evidence of discrimination against other persons of Mexican Nationality or ancestry."

Murrell also gave city officials many examples of discrimination taking place in Slaton through private investigations that had been conducted starting in 1960, including an incident where an investigator was told by the pool manager that the city pool was "whites only." Murrell said they had given Slaton officials plenty of time to correct these issues, but no improvement had been made over the yearlong investigation.

In Article 8 of the Bracero Program, Mexican nationals were to work in areas that were not discriminatory to Mexican people. The Department of Labor had no other options but to rescind the Bracero Program in the area, which would have affected not only Slaton but also the surrounding communities of Lorenzo, Post and Lubbock. The discrimination complaints affected the entire South Plains area, and the discrimination itself, according to Murrell, "applies specifically to the Slaton situation."

By the summer of 1962, when Slaton entered its fifty-first year of existence, the pool was opened to all of Slaton's citizens, no matter their race.

Slaton in '63

It was lunchtime at the Smoot household. After prayer, the Reverend R.M. Smoot and his family sat down to enjoy their lunch in a quiet house, where family discussions took priority over the background noise of television. However, according to the reverend's daughter, Betty Miller, family time was harshly interrupted by the blaring sound of a phone ringing on that Friday afternoon, November 22, 1963.

"My father answered the phone," Betty Miller said in a 1963 article in *The Slatonite*. "I saw him turn white. He managed to tell us what had happened."

Miller said that, for the first time, she saw her father cry.

In another part of town, Conroy Bain was working at the Bain Auto Store and tried his best to focus on the task at hand, helping a customer. On that Friday, however, his thoughts were not of weekend plans or paycheck earnings. A tear formed as he tried maintaining his composure, and his thoughts kept drifting to that tragic event—the assassination of President John F. Kennedy.

"One couldn't help but feel—and hope—that there had been a mistake," Bill Ball reported in *The Slatonite* on November 28, 1963, about the events that had taken place in downtown Dallas earlier that week.

"I'm sorry," Bain told the customer, "but I just can't seem to keep my wits after a terrible thing like this."

"We have lost a great man," he said through tears as he stared out the window onto a beautiful sunny autumn afternoon that followed four days of rain.

All was average in Slaton in '63.

The year began with the annual Chamber of Commerce Banquet, followed by a particularly warm February, and then transitioned into a pleasant spring.

On Saturday, March 30, Tyrone Pawell of Evans High School waited for the results from a panel of judges on a story he had written for the storytelling competition.

He wasn't alone in his wait.

Annie Spencer and Velma Clayton, in their Sunday best, waited for the essays they had carefully crafted in their English classes to be judged as well.

Six other schools competed in the same district as Evans, an all-black school in Slaton, in the District League Academic Meet. The winners of the meet would advance to the state finals at Prairie View A&M University.

When the results were announced, Pawell was at the top of the list; also in first place were the winning essays of Annie Spencer and Velma Clayton. However, they weren't the only students who excelled at the academic meet. Lena Franus Smith took first place in senior spelling, along with Velma Clayton and Richard Kelly. Georgia Hicks won first place in typing. All were students of Evans High School.

After celebrating their district win, the students of Evans High School participated in their usual pomp and circumstance affair of graduation, not knowing that, within two years, the blue and gold gowns of the Evans Wolverines would be traded in for the traditional red gowns of Slaton High School.

The newly integrated pool at the county park was filled with children from all over the community almost every afternoon, weather permitting.

As June made its way into July, the Fourth of July celebration in that same park was honored with a patriotic flyover by supersonic jets.

"A flyover of 16 supersonic T-88 Talon Jet Trainers will include Slaton on a swing made July 4th over 12 South Plains Cities," *The Slatonite* reported. "The Slaton flight will occur at 9:47 am."

For the rest of the summer, as in many other small communities, the talk of the town turned toward pitches, strikes and home runs as the sounds of cheers and the shattering cracks of baseball bats filled the summer air. The Slaton Babe Ruth League All-Stars were up to bat.

On July 18, 1963, *The Slatonite* reported, "The Slaton Babe Ruth League All-Stars defeated Levelland Tuesday night in district play to the tune of 5–4."

The next week, the town cheered on its little hometown heroes in defeating their rival, Post. However, the team's season soon ended after a devastating loss in Tahoka before a large Slaton cheering section.

"The championship game came Saturday evening on the heels of two days of wins for the locals," *The Slatonite* reported in late July of that year. "The final encounter, pitting Slaton against Tahoka in a tight squaker that ended 3–1 favoring the Lynn County boys."

Even a small national news item that affected Slaton greatly took a side note to the pleasant summer. That summer, in June 1963, *The Slatonite* reported that the House of Representatives voted to eliminate the Bracero Program. It was a program that had, for a decade, legally imported Mexican nationals to work in various agricultural ventures.

However, as summer became fall and the sounds of baseball bats cracking to loud hometown Slaton cheers faded, the autumn winds turned, and cold rains flooded the town.

In November, before Thanksgiving, the storms became somewhat violent, and even hail accompanied the rains. For a town whose livelihood depended on agriculture, the rain and hail were not welcomed during what was to be a plentiful harvest.

In mid-autumn of '63, the small-town murmur and chatter of the delinquent rains halted.

The sun shone, and for the people of the town, Friday afternoon, November 22, 1963, was a very pleasant one. The scent of rain lingered, and the air remained humid, but as televisions tuned in to live news broadcasts, the townspeople paused and solemnly watched as John F. Kennedy, their president, was rushed away in a chaotic downtown Dallas scene.

All knew, after that moment, that nothing would be average again.

"It is a terrible thing," Albert Findley said to *The Slatonite*. "It is overwhelming to think, too." His skin glistened in the sun on the town square as he spoke gently, calmly. "To think that President Kennedy visited enemy country without being harmed and then [was] assassinated right here in Texas."

Slaton's Boy, 2009

When it came to the events of November 22, 1963, Charles Truman (C.T.) Walker remained mute. However, his family knew him differently.

"He was a very fun-loving guy," Cecelia Hurst, Walker's cousin, said.

"I'll never forget the day we went to the state fair," Hurst said of her cousin.

> *We got on this giant roller coaster and it went chuch...chuch...chuch all the way to the top and before we knew it, we were flying straight down to the ground. My head was swimming.* [Truman] *asked if we wanted to do it again. That's the kind of guy he was.*

Hurst also said he was the kind of guy she could joke with and laugh till their sides hurt with, and he would, on occasion, take her and their other cousin Dwayne Mounce upstairs in the house he once occupied in Stephenville to tell stories about how the house was haunted.

On November 22, 1963, thirteen-year-old Dwayne Mounce returned home from school to see what the rest of the world was quickly finding out: President John F. Kennedy had been assassinated. "I noticed Oswald, but who I really noticed was C.T.," he said.

Mounce was shocked to see the video image of his cousin, C.T. Walker, flash across the screen as he took accused assassin Lee Harvey Oswald in handcuffs through the panicked downtown streets of Dallas.

"This was our family's fifteen minutes of glory," Mounce said from the Slaton Bakery in 2009. "We just want the people of Slaton to know one of their own sons was a very important part of history."

Walker was born in 1933 in Slaton. His cousin Coy Biggs still resides in Slaton. "C.T. and Coy were very close," Mounce said. "The two bonded very early in life and remained friends even after C.T. moved to Stephenville." The two eventually joined the Coast Guard together, and Walker later began a career in law enforcement. Biggs later served as Lubbock county commissioner.

The events that took place on the day of the assassination have been surrounded by speculation, mystery and, for some, legend.

According to the Warren Commission Report, soon after shooting Kennedy from the sixth floor of the book depository warehouse, where he was an employee, Oswald boarded a bus, which took him to his rooming house to retrieve a jacket. He encountered Patrolman J.D. Tippit on a residential street in the Oak Cliff neighborhood. When Tippit exited his squad car, Oswald shot him four times with a .38-caliber revolver, killing him in view of two witnesses.

In a 1991 article for the *Quinlan-Tawakoni News*, Walker said that as he was leaving the book depository, he heard over his radio that a policeman had been shot. He immediately went to the place where the shooting had occurred.

"I parked behind [Tippit's] vehicle. He was shot outside his car and fell by the left front door. There was so much blood, I knew he couldn't possibly survive," Walker said in the article.

Walker also described the scene that took place downtown as he and his patrolmen tried desperately to find Oswald. The search included a brief chase through alleyways, streets and even the local library: "We searched and checked the library and everyone in it. We had everyone with their hands over their heads, holding shotguns on them. We scared everyone to death."

Walker was still searching when a call came across his scanner, reporting a suspicious man in the Texas Theater.

According to the commission reports, Officer Maurice N. McDonald approached Oswald and ordered him to stand. Soon, McDonald noticed a gun placed within his belt. Walker recalled:

> *McDonald's hand was on the belt of Oswald. Oswald's hand was under it. Then everyone's hands were on his belt. Other officers rushed up and someone yelled for him to let go of the gun. He said, "I can't!" and he couldn't. There were too many hands on him. It looked like a stack of pancakes. Some plainclothesmen got his gun. I handcuffed him, and we took him out.*

In the interview, Walker described Oswald as cold and emotionless as he yelled to the people and reporters who gathered outside the theater. Walker sat in the right rear seat of the police vehicle, the detective sat on the left side and Oswald was in the center as they drove him to the station to be arraigned. He described Oswald as being evasive. "The man had no emotion," Walker said. "We were all nervous wrecks, but he was so calm, no emotion at all. It was spooky calm."

The interview for the *Quinlan-Tawakoni News* is the only interview Walker's family is aware of. "He never told the family a whole lot about what happened that day," Mounce said. "I would try to ask him about the events, but he never really talked about it and always changed the subject. We never knew the details, and we thought we would never know."

Walker's family believed that his story and what took place in the Texas Theater would be carried with him to his grave. Walker died on October 10, 2007, at his home in Tawakoni, Texas.

"Three weeks ago, we discovered this interview," Mounce said of the newspaper article that had been written for the *Quinlan-Tawakoni News*. "We finally got to see his story, and we thought it was fitting to share his legacy with the people of Slaton."

In the article, Walker said he was bombarded by autograph seekers and received a lot of "crazy letters." He also didn't believe any of the conspiracy theories that arose from the incident:

> *Up to the 19th year, every once in a while I was called up to internal affairs and questioned about the events of that day. Rumors were always surfacing and they would question me. On the 19th year I was told that I put in a false report at the library to give Oswald time to get away. I answered, "Yeah and I got 25,000 acres in Cuba, too!" It was so ridiculous and it made me angry! That was the last time I was questioned but I don't think it will ever go away.*

"Like I said," Mounce said, "we never knew the details, and we thought we'd never know. Now, we at least have some closure."

"He was a national hero," Hurst said, "but he never wanted to be. He was just happy being who he was."

The Class of 1968

On a spring afternoon, music drifted from the halls of Slaton High School and out onto the streets when three young Slaton women—Karlene Eastman, Laura Childers and Jo Ann Roberts—sang "Ave Maria" before the graduating class of 1968.

Included in the graduating class was Truett Johnson, whose final quote in the yearbook was: "Men of few words are the best men."

Future Homemakers of America member and choir participant Toni Briseno's final quote for the yearbook was: "From tiny sparks great fires blaze."

Pep squad member Kale Roche wanted everyone to know that "there is a world to see" when she left behind her legacy at Slaton High School.

When the class took to the stage for the final time, it's easy to imagine the graduates thinking back to their childhoods and even their first days of high school as freshmen, in 1964, the first year of integration.

In the summer of '64, however, as new high school freshmen anxiously waited for the first day of school, the carcasses of two hundred white sheep littered the black highway leading into Slaton.

W.M. Young of Lubbock passed through Slaton after visiting with his parents, who lived in Tahoka. As Young, driving a pickup truck, approached the intersection of Highway 400 and the Highway 84 bypass, he slammed on his brakes to avoid smashing into a truck that had failed to acknowledge a stop sign at the intersection before crossing over into the city of Slaton.

"The last thing I remember," Young reported to *The Slatonite* in 1964, "was looking McNeely in the face just as the collision occurred."

When he made the fatal decision to cross the highway without stopping, Clint McNeely was driving a large truck with a guarded trailer attached, carrying approximately six hundred sheep. The four hundred sheep that survived left the carnage and roamed through the streets of Slaton.

They roamed the same streets where, less then a decade earlier, two Slaton police officers had taken part in a high-speed chase, all the while spraying bullets at their culprit.

In a January 1953 article in *The Slatonite*, twenty-nine-year-old Andy Smith lay in critical condition at Mercy Hospital recovering from a gunshot wound.

"Smith was shot in the chest by fellow policeman, Bill White, after the two chased a Negro in a wild car ride from Slaton into downtown Tahoka," *The Slatonite* read in the January 2, 1953 article.

According to the article, White claimed to have walked into an alley between *The Slatonite* office and Brush Motor Freight off Texas Avenue. He strolled past dry brush and graveled grounds in the shadows of the alleyway when he claimed to have seen a "Negro" stealing gas from a pickup truck.

Before the man could respond, a gun was in the air, and White hollered, "Give up or I'll shoot."

After shooting twice, and missing, the man entered the vehicle and drove away. Smith, who was a block away when he heard the gunshots, made his way to the alley, and he and White entered their vehicles and drove onto Texas Avenue, chasing after the man.

"A 90-mile-an-hour car chase ensued all the way to downtown Tahoka," *The Slatonite* reported, "with the police officers and the Negro exchanging shots on the way."

In downtown Tahoka, "the Negro wrecked his car," White said, "and escaped on foot."

White parked the police car, turned to his partner and said, "I'll get him," before exiting the car and chasing the man through the streets of Tahoka.

"White chased the Negro, who zig-zagged between buildings and, at one point, White saw a man, supposedly the Negro, pointing a gun at him," *The Slatonite* reported.

"I thought to myself, it's me or the Negro," White said, "and I shot."

With his gun up, White said he was about to shoot again when he heard the slow, grueling moans of his partner Smith. "It's me, Bill," he said.

"I never felt worse about anything in my life," White reported to *The Slatonite*. "Smith was dressed in civilian clothes and wore no hat. The Negro was also bare headed. I thought Andy was still in the police car or I'd have never taken the chance there in the darkness."

In 1953, those who thought of African Americans as second-class, separate citizens considered racist banter and wit humorous, and these people felt justified in comically satirizing the growing brutality toward African Americans.

Deplorably, *The Slatonite*, too, succumbed to the bigotry of the pre–civil rights years in a humor column for *The Slatonite* entitled "Claude & Irving."

It was the events that transpired after the Chamber of Commerce Banquet that would be the inspiration for the humor column written in a 1953 issue of *The Slatonite*.

"It actually happened," the column began. "Claude and Irving caught a burglar."

"The excitement began for the roly-poly barrister and the lean mustachioed jeweler following the Chamber of Commerce banquet Friday night," the column continued.

As the two men made their way past a jewelry store on 130 North Ninth Street following the banquet, they discovered something unusual about the store's display case: a hole had been made in the display window.

As the two men investigated the scene, they saw a man standing in the alley, and without hesitation, the two sped down the alley in their vehicle toward the man, who ran away on foot.

"There was a Negro whose actions indicated that he was the 'culprit,'" Claude reported to *The Slatonite*.

"Follow that man," Irving shouted to his driver.

The front-page article described the pursuit of the assumed culprit, through alleyways and Slaton streets, as the man being pursued helplessly ran, trying to find safety from the angry men.

The article stated, "The men pursued the Negro by car for a short distance, but realizing that was fruitless, abandoned the vehicle and set after the fleeing Negro on foot."

The police were notified, and they too, without question, searched for the accused assailant. The fleeing man, with nowhere to turn, was cornered at 127 Texas Avenue. The man was arrested and taken away to jail. The heroes of their own story took pride in capturing their "bad guy" as many citizens were entertained by yet another jolly Claude and Irving story.

Two years later, in 1955, the public's fear and the separation of African Americans continued to dominate the front page of *The Slatonite*, where names were rarely given but the term "Negro" continually described members of the community.

That same year, plans began for a new school. It was the school district's hope that the new school, catering to the African American population, would be opened in time for the new school year in 1956. Slaton High School, a whites-only school, was in a brand-new, state-of-the-art facility on the other side of town—less than two miles away.

One month prior to the first day of the new school year, the Slaton School Board voted to maintain segregation within the Slaton Independent School District. "At a meeting of the Slaton School Board," *The Slatonite* reported on August 19, 1955, "a resolution was passed to maintain segregated schools for the school year 1955–56."

At the time, many people in Slaton continued believing that a segregated school system was best for the students in the community. "There had not been enough study of the problem," superintendent of Slaton Public Schools P.C. Vardy Jr. said in *The Slatonite*.

Tragically, in January 1956, eight months before the planned school was to open, a fire ravaged the building of Evans, the all-black school.

"Slaton firemen battled a fire at the Evans School," *The Slatonite* reported in 1956. The children, left without a school, were placed in various other locations throughout the town, even though a brand-new Slaton High School with new amenities and plenty of space was just a few yards away.

"The new Evans School which had previously been planned, is expected to be ready in September," *The Slatonite* reported.

The students would be separated by race for the next nine years. The students of Latin descent were separated by skin tones; the dark-skinned Latino students were required to attend Evans, while the light-skinned Latino students attended Slaton High School. Since most towns in the area did not have an "all-black high school," black students from neighboring communities and towns also attended Evans.

However, the Civil Rights Act of 1964 changed the face of the Slaton school system.

In August 1964, Slaton Independent School District announced its plans to begin integrating the entire district, beginning with the junior and senior classes and continuing each year to make accommodations for all schools to be integrated.

That same summer, the summer when hundreds of sheep ran loose in the streets of Slaton, two young men from different sides of town followed the sounds of sheep cries and made their way to the scene of the accident.

The two met as they aided a sheep lying on the ground, still breathing, when so many others had died.

"Two unidentified youths made an attempt to save an exhausted sheep that was many of hundreds involved in the truck accident Saturday afternoon," *The Slatonite* reported.

A week after the roaming herd was caught and the blood of the sheep was cleansed, the two youths entered the same school, not as separate members of one town but as equals.

In May 1965, school officials reported to *The Slatonite*, "The final copy of our integration plans, which were formulated in September, 1964, will be sent to Washington D.C."

Before the school year began in August 1965, a small news item directed to the parents of Slaton students read, "Buses will begin operation Monday. Routes remain the same as last school year with the exception that children of all races will ride the same buses."

After the graduating class of 1968 walked the stage and the young Slaton women sang "Ava Maria," the students of all different ethnicities—black, white and brown—threw their mortar caps high into the air.

For a brief moment, the signature school color, Slaton red, reigned.

Coffee Talk at the Auto Shop, 2009

As the dog days of summer lingered a few weeks longer, on one unpleasantly hot and dry August afternoon in Slaton, a group of men met behind the tools and vehicle parts of O.D. Kenney Auto Shop.

The men have met every day "since O.D. Kenney himself was serving the coffee," the self-appointed leader of the group, William, said as five other men sat silently, nodding their heads. "Now, don't let 'em fool ya," he said. "He goes there, he goes there and he goes there." William pointed out the silent patrons.

The silence didn't last much longer.

When asked why the daily meetings over the past forty-plus years were held, William quickly responded, "For the free coffee."

The group of men also said they enjoy the pleasant conversations of weather, farming, the railroad "and sometimes the golf course," one of the men added.

"They closed down the golf course," another man replied.

"See, this is where I find everything out," the first man responds.

Some of the topics not discussed, however, are politics and religion. "We just don't discuss that," William said, "there's enough of that everywhere else."

On this day, the group consisted of William, Ed, Franklin, Donald, Joe and Charles. Ed, William and Franklin were members of the Slaton High School class of 1950; Donald belonged to the class of 1953; and Joe graduated in 1954. Charles was a member of the Wilson High School class of 1960. "He's the young one," Joe said of Charles.

O.D. Kenney Auto Store is one of Slaton's oldest businesses, opened in 1929. *Photo from the Alton Kenney collection.*

For most of the meetings, the men sit and remember the past. "I remember all of the trees," Joe said.

"If you walked down the streets," William remembered, "you'd be in the shade most of the time."

The men spend most of their time throwing around names and remembering past friends. Such memories include the year that bright yellow school buses first traveled the streets of Slaton.

"We were juniors in high school," William said. "When Slaton got school busses it was 1948." He said the buses were lined with images of the Cleveland Indians baseball team. It was also a time when Slaton's football rival was Lubbock High School.

The men also remembered when a hamburger stand sat across the street from the high school, which was once the current junior high building. "You could get a hamburger for a quarter," William said.

"I couldn't," Franklin chimed in. "We were so poor, I had to take lunch in a beat-up old bag."

"Yeah," William said. "We talk about how poor we were; we were so poor we spelled it with three *O*s."

When not joking about the past, the group took a moment to discuss the present, which included children, grandchildren, the occasional divorce and even death. "If you miss [a meeting,] something's wrong," William said. "We talk about a lot of illness."

A brief silence followed William's statement before Joe spoke up. "Or we just say he took too many Viagras," he said.

The group, although discussing current issues for a brief moment, chose to remain vigilant of the past.

"We lived through the biggest changes that ever happened in the world," Joe said.

Joe remembered watching *Sputnik* launch and said, "I remember thinking that the world was never going to be the same."

The men also remembered the turbulent 1960s—the Vietnam era, free love and civil rights. "The civil rights movement changed the United States more than anything else," Joe said. "At the time, the kids at Evans High School"—the exclusively black school—"were urged to come over."

William remembered when a special assembly was held at the school during the integration era. "I remember we were all rowdy," he said. "A little

A postcard promoting the city of Slaton in 1910. *Photo from the Slaton Town Square Antique Mall and Museum.*

black girl stood and quieted us by reciting the Emancipation Proclamation. We were all stunned."

The men said that although the changes that have occurred in their lives were historic and monumental, they are never too old to learn new things. "You know," William said, "even though I was against integration, I have lived my whole life just to realize how wrong I was."

The men said they would continue to meet every day through rain or shine, sleet or snow—and even during the blistering dog days of summer.

Index

A

Abel, Tom 75
Adams, Julia Ann Price 71, 72, 74, 77, 95
Adams, Sam Houston, Dr. 22, 24, 56, 70, 71, 72, 73, 74, 75, 76, 77, 78, 79, 88, 95
Amarillo, Texas 47, 49, 64
American Academy of Dramatic Arts 74
Atchison, Topeka and Santa Fe Railroad 72
Austin, Texas 63, 64, 65
Ayers, Ray C. 103

B

Bain, Conroy 122
Ball, Bill 122
Baxley, Onie 16
Beal, C.B. 63
Beal, S.W., Dr. 63
Biggs, Coy 126
Blossom, Texas 85
Boyle, H.H. 113
Boy Scouts of America 114
Bracero Program 111, 121, 124
Brasfield, Earl 103
Brennan Construction Company 64
Brennan, Joe 64
Brewer, J.H. 62
Brewer, Verna Dale 35
Brighton, Wisconsin 51
Briseno, Toni 128
Brush Motor Freight 129
Bryant, Willie 39
Buenger, Walter 53
Buffalo Lake 120
Burlington, Wisconsin 51
Burns, P.J. 114

C

Cabrera, Frances 90
Caldwell Farm 110
Canton, Texas 103
Capps Hotel 28, 37
Caprock Pharmacy 28
Carter, J. Michael 47, 49
Case, J.I. 20
Castleberry, Doc 37
chamber of commerce 26, 35, 64, 101, 114, 123, 130

C.H. Fawcett Confectionary 26
Childers, Laura 128
City Hall, Slaton 61
Civic and Culture Club 35, 94, 95
civil rights 34, 130, 131, 135
civil rights movement 34, 135
Claude & Irving 130
Clayton, Velma 123
Cleveland Indians 134
Crosby County 94
Custer, Jeff 53

D

Dallas, Texas 13, 46, 64, 122, 124, 125
Darwin, Ray 58, 61
Davis, Ben 120
Davis, Robert Hall 114
Deering, Bonnie Abel 41
Del Rio, Texas 83
Diaz, Ben 109, 110
Diaz, Ignacio 109
Diaz, Jesus 109
Diaz, Joe 109
Diaz, Juanita 109
Diaz, Librado 109
Diaz, Moses 109
Diaz, Sara 109
Doherty, Clyde 115
Duncan, Oklahoma 35
Dust Bowl 58

E

Eastman, Karlene 128
East Ward School 60, 62, 103
Echer, Brooksie Nell 75
Elliot, James Arthur 35
Elliot, Sarah Callhan 35
Emancipation Proclamation 85, 136
Englewood Cemetery 78, 80, 87, 88, 89
English, Pauline Margaret 82
Englund, Bud 88
Englund, Dubbin 88
Englund, Glynna 88
Englund, Robert 58, 88
Enloe, Mary 59, 99
Evans High School 123, 135

F

Fields, Edith 84
First Baptist Church 38, 40
First State Bank 35, 62, 63
Flores, Ysaura 90
Forrest Hotel 28, 113, 114, 115
Fort Worth, Texas 62, 74
Foster, E.C. 87

G

Garza County 94
Germany 46, 47, 68
Golden Anniversary 119
Gonzales, Joe 91
Great Depression 55, 56
Great Plains 58, 60, 66, 109
Green, Lowell C. 19, 21

H

Hamlin Supply 41
Hardesty, John Peddigrew 38, 42, 45, 48
Harley Sadler Tent Show 103
Harvey House 67
Harvey, Michelle 49
Haverman, L.B. 114
Herman, Jesse 35
Hermleigh, Texas 46
Hernandez, Delfina 109
Hickman, R.D. 107
Hicks, Georgia 123
High School, Slaton 62, 88, 119, 123, 128, 131, 133

Hilders, F.J. 75, 77
Hillenbrand, Fredrick J. 51
Hill, Pearlie 84, 85
Hodge, Dora F. Johnson 35, 36
Hoffman, A.L. 46
Holly, Buddy 100
Hood, Odie 101
Howell, Rebecca Diane 107
Howerton, A.E. 87
Hubbard, Vyola 21, 22, 67
Hurst, Cecelia 125

I

Illinois, Chicago 21
integration 128, 132, 135, 136
Iowa, Onawa 29
Itty Bitty Drug 115

J

J.H. Teague & Son, Confections, Drug Sundries 40
Jim Crow laws 89, 110
Johnson, Deacon Aren 39
Johnson, Louise 84
Johnson, Reuben 39
Johnson, Truett 128
Jones, Arthur 39

K

Kaiser 47
Keller, Father Joseph M. 45, 46, 51
Kelly, Richards 123
Kennedy, President John F. 122, 124, 125
Kern, Mary Belle 29
Kerrigan, Francis Adams 70
Keys, R.A. 63, 65
Klattenhoff, M.F. 46
Klattenhoff, W.J. 89
Koch, Fred 64
Kokernot, H.L. 20
Kokernot, J.W. 20
Korn, Oscar 53
Ku Klux Klan 40, 50

L

Lamb, Brad 107
Lamesa, Texas 62, 99
Lane, Julia Alice Florence 61
Laredo, Texas 90
Lorenzo, Texas 121
Lubbock Avalanche-Journal 67, 75, 78
Lubbock, Texas 21, 23, 25, 28, 29, 41, 42, 49, 56, 67, 68, 69, 75, 78, 82, 89, 94, 99, 100, 101, 103, 104, 113, 121, 126, 128, 134

M

Maxey's Café 108
McCormick, Johnny 105
McDonald, Maurice N. 126
McKinnon, K.S. 103
McNeely, Clint 129
Meeks, Alton 97, 100
Meeks, Mary Helen 97
Meeks, Roy 97
Meeks, Sue 97
Mercy Center 31
Mercy Hospital 63, 64, 66, 129
Methodist Church 43, 73
Mexican Revolution 90
Mexico 36, 90, 109
Miller, Betty 122
Miss Slaton 119
Monahans, Texas 53
Moore Confectionary 26
Mounce, Dwayne 125
Mt. Olive Baptist Church 40
Murrell, Tracy O. 120

N

Nazi 108
Nebraska 109, 110
Nesbitt, J.W. 75, 78
New York City 22, 74
Nichols, E.O., Dr. 22, 23, 24

O

Obrian, J.W. 87
Odd Fellows Hall 48
O.D. Kenney Auto Shop 133
Oswald, Lee Harvey 125, 126, 127
Our Lady of Guadalupe 91

P

Palace Theater 53
Pavehouse, H.M. 81
Pawell, Tyrone 123
Pearl Harbor 82, 100, 105
Pecos River 93
Pember, Bruce 26, 29
Pember Hide and Fur House 29
Pember, Joyce Cheatham 29
Pember, Lillian 26, 28
Pember, Merritt 29, 30
Pember, Royce 26, 101
Phillips, J.C. 20
Pioneer Days 100
Plainview, Texas 72
Post, Texas 97, 121, 124
Potters' Field 87, 89
Prairie View A&M University 123
Presbyterian Church 111
Privett, Mary Grace 60

Q

Quinlan-Tawakoni News 126, 127

R

Railroad Avenue 34
Red Cross 23, 94
Red River War 85
Reed, Ragan 75
Reid, D.R. 100
Reisdorff, Father Joseph 38
Rhoades, Carolyn 119
Ridley, A.D. 84, 85
Roberts, Jo Ann 128
Robertson, A.B. 93
Robertson, Briggs 102
Robertson, Emma Lenorah 93
Roche, Kale 128
Rogers, W.H. 101
Roosevelt, Eleanor 95

S

Santa Fe Depot 102
Santa Fe Railroad 34, 38, 41
Santa Fe Railway 20, 21, 88
Santa Fe Railway Company 20, 21
Santa Fe Reading Room 36
Schuette, Annie 31, 32, 33, 59, 60, 61, 65, 66
Scott, Cecil 69, 81
Scudder, K.L. 111
Selman, Sam 52
Shankle, Robert 58
Shorty Mell's Café 108
Simancher, Frank 46
Simpson, Jimella Wilson 107
Singleton Hotel 28, 81
Sisters of Mercy 38, 50, 64
Skull and Crossbones 43, 44
Slaton Babe Ruth League All-Stars 123
Slaton Bakery 23, 102, 105, 106, 107, 125
Slaton Care Center 16, 31, 97, 100
Slaton City Line Home Demonstration Club 58
Slaton Club House 32, 113, 114
Slaton Co-op Gin 99

Slatonite, The 19, 38, 43, 46, 47, 53, 62, 63, 64, 65, 67, 69, 84, 85, 94, 95, 96, 100, 101, 102, 104, 113, 114, 115, 119, 120, 121, 122, 123, 124, 128, 129, 130, 131, 132
Slaton, O.L. 21
Slaton Power and Light Company 35
Slaton Power Plant 34
Slaton Salvage Committee 100
Slaton's Story 26, 30, 35, 36, 37, 38, 42, 43, 46, 47, 58, 60, 61, 62, 63, 64, 67, 70, 71, 74, 87, 88, 89, 93, 94, 97, 103, 104, 107, 109, 111
Slaton Theater 62, 110
Slaton Town Square 37, 40, 52, 75, 113, 119
Sledge, Bill 29
Sledge, Melvin 29, 57
Sledge, Victor Cade 29
Slone, Luke 111
Smallwood, Dana Ross 103
Smith, Andy 129
Smith, Jeanna 81
Smith, Lena Franus 123
Smoothies, The 120
Smoot, R.M. 122
Spencer, Annie 123
Sputnik 135
Stanton, Texas 64
State Baptist Convention 38
St. Charles Borromeo 51
Stephen F. Austin Elementary 103
Stilson, Eli 20
St. Joseph Catholic Church 38, 39, 45, 50, 64
Stone, C.L. 81
Storey, E.B., Jr. 21
Supreme Feed Mills 103

T

Tahoka, Texas 124, 128, 129
Talley, H.D. 69
Taylor, Texas 109
Teague, Joe, Sr. 41
Terry, Lula Lee 85
Texas, Amarillo 19
Texas Avenue 26, 28, 87, 94, 105, 108, 129, 130
Texas, Dallas 88
Texas, Fort Worth 61
Texas History Handbook 60
Texas-Indian Wars 85
Texas, Lamesa 62
Texas, Lubbock 36, 72
Texas, State of 20
Texas Technological College 68
Texas Tech University 69, 88
Texas Theater 126, 127
Texas Utilities Company 36
Texas, Wilson 29
Texas Women's College 74
Thorndale, Texas 110
Tiger Stadium 99, 120
Tippit, J.D. 126
Tubbs, Walter L. 38
Tudor, Muriel 62
Tudor, R.H. 62
Tudor, R.L. 74, 75, 78, 80
Tudor, Woodie 74, 78, 79, 80

U

University Medical Center 49
U.S. Department of Labor 120
USO reading room 101
Utter, J.F. 19

V

Van Zandt County 103
Vardy, P.C., Jr. 131
VFW Hall 120

Vickers, J.E. 77
Vietnam 55, 135

W

Waldrop, John Emmett 37
Walker, C.T. 125
Walston, Opal Mosley 62, 63
Walter, Adolph 56
Walter, Melvin 55
Warren Commission Report 126
Washington, D.C. 21, 83, 132
Webb Confectionary 26
Westefeld, Josephine Scott Adams 70
Western Land and Livestock Company 20
White, Bill 129
Wicker, R.L. 58
Wilborn, Oscar Sr. 39
Williams, Floyd 52
Williams, Webber Beauregard 88
Wilselman Theater 52
Wilson, Barney 105
Wilson, Max 106
Wilson, Ollie Mae 107
World War I 31, 35, 46, 47, 55, 90
World War II 82, 103, 105, 108, 110, 111

Y

Yeager, Georgia Mae 75
Young, W.M. 128

About the Author

James Villanueva is a graduate of Eastern New Mexico University. His writing has been featured in *Texas Monthly* magazine, *Go* magazine, the *Lubbock Avalanche-Journal*, *Latino Lubbock Magazine* and *Texas Escapes Online*. He was an events and education administrator for the Buddy Holly Center and the Silent Wings Museum in Lubbock. He is now a staff writer for *The Slatonite*.

Photo by Jackye Neal.